# Fulfilling Love

*From Sin to Surrender*

Stacey Lynn

WestBow
PRESS
A DIVISION OF THOMAS NELSON

WestBow Press books may be ordered through booksellers or by contacting:

WestBow Press
A Division of Thomas Nelson
1663 Liberty Drive
Bloomington, IN 47403
www.westbowpress.com
1-(866) 928-1240

Because of the dynamic nature of the Internet, any web addresses or links contained in this book may have changed since publication and may no longer be valid. The views expressed in this work are solely those of the author and do not necessarily reflect the views of the publisher, and the publisher hereby disclaims any responsibility for them.

Any people depicted in stock imagery provided by Thinkstock are models, and such images are being used for illustrative purposes only.

Certain stock imagery © Thinkstock.

ISBN:  978-1-4497-7531-5 (sc)
ISBN:  978-1-4497-7532-2 (hc)
ISBN:  978-1-4497-7530-8 (e)

Library of Congress Control Number: 2012922245

Printed in the United States of America

WestBow Press rev. date: 11/20/2012

*I say then: Walk in the Spirit,*

*and you shall not fulfill the lust of the flesh.*

Galatians 5:16 *(NKJV)*


**This is all for Him--**

**Jesus Christ, my Lord and Savior.**

I traveled to the depths of darkness

And He never left my side.

He is my best friend,

And He is the lover of my soul.


Editor – Jan Romeo

Artwork Design – Raydean Borchers & Jordan Heep

# CONTENTS

# Introduction

As I settle in at the computer to begin typing my story, my heart is racing. I have been thinking about sharing this story--my life--for years. Last year, before I put any thoughts on paper, the Lord spoke to me saying, "I want you to give details. I want you to share the *details* of your testimony." Our Lord is interested in the details of our lives. He sees and knows everything. He brought to my remembrance the story of the woman at the well.

*Jesus said to her, "Go, call your husband, and come here." The woman answered and said, "I have no husband." Jesus said to her, "You have well said, 'I have no husband,' " "for you have had five husbands, and the one whom you now have is not your husband; in that you spoke truly." The woman said to Him, "Sir, I perceive that You are a prophet."* John 4:16-19 *(NKJV)*

Jesus was very specific with this woman concerning her sin. He cited details of her life to her. He did not condemn her, but He shared the truths of her life with her. The Lord also directed me to David and Bathsheba.

*Then it happened one evening that David arose from his bed and walked on the roof of the king's house. And from the roof he saw a woman bathing, and the woman was very beautiful to behold. So David sent and inquired about the woman. And someone said, "Is this not Bathsheba, the daughter of Eliam, the wife of Uriah the Hittite?" Then David sent messengers, and took her; and she came to him, and he lay with her, for she was cleansed from her impurity; and she returned to her house. And the woman conceived; so she sent and told David, and said, "I am with child."* 2 Sam 11:2-5 *(NKJV)*

The Word clearly identifies for us the sins that David committed: Lusting, coveting, adultery. The verses that follow (2 Sam 11:8-15) illustrate a downward spiral of sin in David's life. He devised a deceptive scheme attempting to cover the first sins and when it didn't work he purposefully arranged for Bathsheba's husband to be killed, thus adding the sins of lying and murder to his rap sheet. Again, God's Word identifies the specifics of these sins, even though we know David did repent of his sins, and we are assured in The Word that his sins were completely forgiven.

*Have mercy upon me, O God, according to Your lovingkindness; according to the multitude of Your tender mercies, blot out my transgressions. Wash me thoroughly from my iniquity, and cleanse me from my sin. For I acknowledge my transgressions, and my sin is always before me. Against You, You only, have I sinned, and done this evil in Your sight-- that You may be found just when You speak, and blameless when You judge.* Psalms 51:1-4 *(NKJV)*

*Purge me with hyssop, and I shall be clean; wash me, and I shall be whiter than snow. Make me to hear joy and gladness, that the bones You have broken may rejoice. Hide Your face from my sins, and blot out all my iniquities. Create in me a clean heart, O God, and renew a steadfast spirit within me. Do not cast me away from Your presence, and do not take Your Holy Spirit from me. Restore to me the joy of Your salvation, and uphold me by Your generous Spirit.* Psalms 51:7-12 *(NKJV)*

And why does God give us the details of David's mistakes—his sins? To show us His marvelous grace; to show us that though we sin and often fall short of the glory of God, yet He is willing and able to give us, as He gave David, a clean heart and a renewed spirit. The Lord showed us David's heart of repentance in order that we would be able to see the complete forgiveness that our Lord God bestows upon all repentant sinners. Despite these and other sins he committed, David was known as a man after God's own heart; and whatever we have done, we also can be restored, or brought anew, to the same closeness to God that David enjoyed. Indeed, the Bible is filled with stories of failures and sins in the lives of past saints. Instead of ignoring or minimizing them, The Word of God uses those mistakes, those sins, to teach and guide us.

In much the same way, the Lord has directed me to write my story, so it can be a teaching tool for others. He has called me to share specifics of the downward spiral of sexual sin that evolved in my life. Today's Christian church is very "hush hush" concerning sexual sin. Many feel that it's unnecessary to discuss such sins. I truly believe that the Lord is calling me to address this issue because there are many Christian women in our modern, very secular world who are feeling trapped in sexual sin. They feel that they cannot speak about this with other Christian women and that no one will understand the bondage they are in. They are ashamed of the desires that their flesh is having, and often they do not understand how this could even be happening to them because they are Christians.

There are also women who do not know Jesus Christ as their personal Lord and Savior yet, and who are trapped in sexual sin. They also feel there is no one to talk to--no one who could possibly understand their pain. They may desire to come to church but they are afraid and ashamed. They feel that Christians will judge them and look down on them for this type of sin. These women often find that the Church doesn't talk about sexual sin, except to say, "Don't do it." Oh, once in a while at church we may hear someone say that she was, or is, in sexual sin. "I was trapped in sexual sin, but now I have been set free," she might proclaim in relief. I praise God for that, and I would never minimize the healing reflected in those words because being set free is amazing. Having those chains broken In Jesus Name is marvelous.

*"Therefore if the Son makes you free, you shall be free indeed.* John 8:36 *(NKJV)*

But what about the woman who has not been set free? What about the woman who comes for prayer, and, if she is bold enough, whispers, "Please pray for me, I am struggling with sexual sin." How do we help her? We say a quick prayer for her and she returns to her seat. Then she leaves the church service, goes back home, and inside of her soul she is still yearning for help. She is screaming inside, trying to understand what has taken place in her life. She needs wisdom, knowledge, and understanding from the Word of God, in order for her chains to be broken.

I have learned that it is very difficult for a woman to share with others that she is trapped in sexual sin. I believe one of the main reasons for this is that from a worldly standpoint, sexual sin is a man's sin. As a culture, we believe that women do not become addicted to sex; that women do not enjoy watching pornography; that women do not and could not crave sex all the time. Because that's what the world believes, a woman, especially a Christian woman, who is trapped in sexual sin, is probably not going to tell anyone about it. Who could understand such a thing? How could such a thing even happen? How could she come and tell the Church when the Church hardly ever speaks of sexual sin? The Church, overall, does not feel comfortable with the topic of sex. In most churches, everyone begins to cringe and squirm in their seats as soon as the subject of "sex" is mentioned.

As a result, the woman living in sexual bondage feels completely helpless and feels that there's no escape. She is trapped, wrapped in chains, and she is involved in sin so deeply that she can barely breathe. That was my story. I was a small-town Christian girl who, as a teenager, loved the Lord deeply. So how did I end up at age twenty-seven, married, and yet in complete, and total sexual bondage? How did I enter into sexual perversion? How could this happen? How could this happen to a Christian? It can happen. It did happen. And as I share with you the details of how it happened, I earnestly pray that the Lord will use my story to help set women free from bondage to sexual sin, and to prevent other women from ever going down this road.

I will be sharing with you the downward spiral of sexual sin that occurred in my life. Much like a mischievous little puppy, sexual sin seems like something that couldn't ever cause any real harm. Though it begins as something simply gratifying to the flesh, it ends up completely destroying your very life. It is very dangerous. Do not be deceived, puppies grow and so does sin. Things that seemed fairly harmless at the start led me down a path that I never could have imagined. That puppy grew into a ravenous, ferocious wolf. I went to the edge of hell and dangled my feet there. And the craziest, most wonderful thing is that Jesus went with me! He promised that He will never leave us or forsake us. I love Him so much because He never abandoned me in my sin. When I walked in darkness, He walked with me.

Thanks be to God that though my sins were as scarlet, I am now as white as snow. I am the Bride of Christ. I am pure and holy in His eyes. I am forgiven and He has cast my sins as far as the East is from the West. My chains are gone. He set me free. He can also set you free, and heal you completely.

You may be thinking that you are nowhere near being in sexual bondage. You may be thinking this book is not something that you need to even read. Before you put this book down, here are a few questions that I would like for you to consider:

1. Have you ever had a lustful thought toward someone?

2. Are you having sexual relations outside of marriage?

3. Are you having ungodly sex in your marriage? Yes, this is possible. My sexual bondage began in my marriage bed.

4. Have you ever done something sexually that you did not want to do but that someone talked you into? Is your husband talking you into doing things that you do not want to do?

5. Do you know someone who is sexually promiscuous, who you do not understand nor know how to help?

6. Are you in a position of leadership among women and not understand what a stronghold sin is?

If you answered "yes" to any of these questions, then please *read this book*; I believe you will find it helpful and enlightening.

Before you step out into sexual sin, any sin for that matter, you first think about it; everything starts in your mind. My pastor says, "Battles are won or lost in the mind." If you are in this battle right now, you can have victory in Jesus Christ. As my story unfolds, you will see the destruction that this sin causes. But in the end, you will see the deliverance and the power that Jesus Christ gives.

*Therefore, if anyone is in Christ, he is a new creation; old things have passed away; behold, all things have become new. Now all things are of God, who has reconciled us to Himself through Jesus Christ, and has given us the ministry of reconciliation, that is, that God was in Christ reconciling the world to Himself, not imputing their trespasses to them, and has committed to us the word of reconciliation. Now then, we are ambassadors for Christ, as though God were pleading through us: we implore you on Christ's behalf, be reconciled to God. For He made Him who knew no sin to be sin for us, that we might become the righteousness of God in Him.* 2 Corinthians 5:17-21 *(NKJV)*

Before I begin the story, I want to assure you that none of the things that I did are someone else's fault. *My* sin is *my* fault. I cannot blame my sinning on anyone else. I may have been lured or enticed, but I am the one to blame for stepping out into sin. I was not forced to do the things I did. I choose to do them; maybe reluctantly at times, but in the end, my sin was my choice. Do not blame my sin on anyone else; that is the last thing that I want to see happen with this book. And I ask you, reader, not to ever blame your sin on someone else.

I ended up in great sin because I did not stand strong in my faith. I did not stand in what I knew to be the truth. I will stand alone before my God, as I am responsible for this life that I have lived. Actually, I will not be standing there all alone. Jesus Christ my Savior will be there with me and He did choose to take on the responsibility of my sin. I am covered in His Blood and my God will not see my sin on me. God is my judge and no one else.

*My little children, these things I write to you, so that you may not sin. And if anyone sins, we have an Advocate with the Father, Jesus Christ the righteous. And He Himself is the propitiation for our sins, and not for ours only but also for the whole world.* I Jonn 2:1-2 *(NKJ)*

Also, as we begin this journey concerning my downward spiral of sexual sin, I want to assure you that writing and re-living this have not been easy for me. For years and years I did forget those things which I had done, those things which were behind me. I pressed forward toward Christ, toward maturity in Him and toward His goal for me. At this point in time, pressing forward in Him has led me to reach out to someone in need, perhaps you, by sharing my story. And I found encouragement in The Word of God:

*Brethren, I do not count myself to have apprehended; but one thing I do, forgetting those things which are behind and reaching forward to those things which are ahead, I press toward the goal for the prize of the upward call of God in Christ Jesus.* Philippians 3:13-14 *(NKJV)*

As I began transcribing my story, at times I felt the urge to leave out some events and facts. As I was contemplating doing that, the Lord spoke one single word to me. His still, small voice said, "Details."

At that very moment, I dropped to my knees and began sobbing as I realized that the road I was about to travel in opening up my heart to you was not going to be pleasant. But it is true, and Truth is always victorious. All who know me well know that I shout Truth from the depths of my soul. Jesus is my *everything*, and He conquered this sin in my life. He will conquer the sin in your life too.

Finally, let me assure you that as I share the details of my sin, I am not going to be graphic about these events. Sexual sin has no glamour to it at all. It is evil, and that is how I will portray each one of these sins for you. I only mention the kinds of things I have done for your understanding; I won't dwell on those activities.

# ONE

## Innocence

My downward spiral of sexual sin occurred mostly during my twenties; but in order for you to appreciate the full scope of my experience you must know where I started the journey. Sexual sin began in my teen years, as it did for so many \living in our world since the so-called Sexual Revolution of the 1960s. From my very innocent childhood I evolved into a teenager not unlike most teens who, when they think they are in love, also think they are responsible and mature enough to handle a physical relationship.

## Junior High

It was the summer before my eighth grade year and I had never had a boyfriend. After all, I was only thirteen years old. I had had those typical puppy-love crushes on a few guys, but I never "went out" with any of them. Nobody went anywhere anyway, at that age.

I attended Sunday school and church on a regular basis at the First Baptist Church in my town. That summer our church built a Family Life Center and I was there all of the time. I have always enjoyed sports, so I was jogging around the track, playing basketball, and playing racquetball almost every day. My relationship with the Lord was in a very young stage. I would pray to Him and read a chapter of His Word almost every night.

One day while I was at the Center I noticed a particular guy, a high school student, who grabbed my attention. He was sixteen and we began talking to one another. His name was Scott. The sparks were there, and before I had a chance to think about it, we were hanging out together often at the Center. One night as he was getting ready to leave the center

I walked outside with him to say good-bye. We were just talking in the parking lot. I will never forget that evening because it was then that I received my first kiss. It may sound nice, but believe it or not, the night ended with this so-very-naïve girl (me) in utter tears. Let me explain.

As Scott and I were talking in the parking lot, one of my cousins walked out of the building to his car. He greeted us, and then drove off. Scott and I continued talking, and then all of a sudden Scott leaned over and kissed me. It was completely unexpected for me. Suddenly I was being kissed and I didn't know what to do. I didn't know what to say to him. Abruptly, and silently, I walked back into the Family Life Center building.

Soon my sister and I left the Center to give another of my cousins a ride home. When we got to his house the cousin who had seen me in the parking lot with Scott approached me. He scolded me for having been out in the parking lot alone with Scott; my parents would not have approved of that he insisted. I was already feeling uncomfortable about the unexpected kiss, and now I was feeling guilty. By the time I walked into my own house, I broke down and cried in my dad's arms, telling him what had occurred.

The next day was Sunday and I saw Scott at church. Not knowing what to say or how to act, I didn't even speak to him. My summer "romance" came to a hasty end without any discussion. I realize my actions sound very childish…and that's because *I was a child*.

Why am I going into such great detail of my first kiss? To illustrate what a tender heart I had at age thirteen and to show you that I began my romantic life from a place of purity and innocence.

By the time I started eighth grade at age fourteen it seemed that all of my friends had boyfriends. When track season arrived a guy named Dillon asked me if I wanted to "go with him." Of course we weren't *going* anywhere, that's just what we called it. So Dillon and I started going together, and we spent hours talking together on the phone. This was puppy-love and I really liked Dillon a lot. Everything was great until one of my friends invited us to a dance at her house. I knew what that meant: I had been to dances at other friends' homes, and I knew that if I went to the dance with Dillon, he would kiss me. The thought of that was just too much for me, so I did the only thing that I could think of to do--I broke up with him. I laugh now while typing this, but I wasn't laughing then, and neither was Dillon. We were good friends. Nothing had happened. He could not understand why I was breaking up with him. I could not tell him that I was not ready to be kissed. All of my friends were kissing, but just the thought of it made me feel very anxious.

By the end of my eighth grade year I was definitely falling in love with my precious Savior. I had been talking to God for months, and even reading His Word, but on Father's Day that year I asked Jesus Christ to come and live inside of me, to be my Lord and Savior in a personal way. From that point on Jesus was a very important part of my life; indeed He was becoming my life. I read His Word almost every day and I prayed to Him on a regular basis. I was involved in my youth group, and I felt my life was going really well.

*You will show me the path of life; in Your presence is fullness of joy; at Your right hand are pleasures forevermore.* Psalms 16:11 *(NKJV)*

# High School

High school rolled around and there I was, still without a boyfriend. I thought of Scott often (my first kiss – my only kiss at this point) and now I was going to be at the same school with him. I was a freshman and he was a senior. I also saw him at my church a lot, but we had not spoken for a very long time. It was in the spring of my ninth grade year that I began talking to him again. I had always liked him since that summer at the Family Life Center, but I had kept my distance from him. Now, however, I felt that I was ready for a relationship with him. I knew that he had had a few girlfriends over the past few years, but I was aware that he did not have one right then. So, we became reacquainted.

We began spending time together, and one night at the Family Life Center, Scott asked me if he could kiss me. I guess he had learned something from what had happened the first time he kissed me. I told him that he could, and this time I didn't freak out about it. We began dating and we began to fall in love. We went to church together and we were definitely high school sweethearts. He was my first real boyfriend.

I will never forget my mom attempting to talk to me one night. You know, the "birds and the bees" talk. I told her that I did not need that talk. I told her that I knew everything about sex. She laughed and she really tried to have this conversation with me, but I kept telling her I knew all about sex and that I could handle it. Oh my goodness, I knew nothing! I knew there was kissing and I knew there was intercourse, but that's all I knew. Seriously, at age fifteen, I thought there was nothing else to know.

None of my youth leaders at church ever talked about sex. They would say that sex before marriage was wrong, and that it's a sin, but I thought they only meant sexual intercourse because that was the only sex that I knew about. Nothing was ever mentioned at my youth group about things like petting or oral sex. I realize those words should not be said in a group setting, but in my opinion, since our public schools are teaching teens about sex, and since the world just assumes teens know all about sex, then the church should definitely be teaching teens about sex (of course with permission of the parents). In fact, the best thing would be for the parents to teach their own children, or at least accompany their teens to a youth group that is teaching about God's will for sexual relations. Ideally the Church should separate the young men from the young ladies, and teach them the truths in God's Word concerning sexual relations and sexual sin.

I wish that I had let my mom speak to me that night. I know she would have given me such wisdom, but I closed her off. Unfortunately, I can't change what happened, but I can learn from my mistakes and move forward. You can be certain that I have talked about God's will for sex with my four daughters very openly, and I did not wait for them to have boyfriends. I wanted them to know ahead of time about sex, before they were confronted with that temptation. I wanted them to know that all sex outside of marriage is a sin, and I wanted them to know the range of behaviors that are all a part of "having sex."

My innocence of sexual things was a major disadvantage for me. With Scott, when kissing led to other things, I did not even know what was really happening. I just allowed him to do these things to me, and I honestly did not know they were sin. I knew sexual intercourse was a sin, but I didn't realize that making out very passionately and placing hands in certain places was sin. It seemed harmless to me at the time, and I was really falling in love with him; making out seemed like the natural thing to do. It *was* the natural thing to do for my flesh, but what was happening to my spirit? I didn't realize it at the time, but my spirit was becoming weaker and my flesh was becoming stronger.

*For the flesh lusts against the Spirit, and the Spirit against the flesh; and these are contrary to one another, so that you do not do the things that you wish.* Galatians 5:17 *(NKJV)*

I will never forget one particular afternoon when I was in the tenth grade; that afternoon I did something sexually that I did not want to do. I did it because I allowed myself to be talked into it. I did it to please Scott, even though every fiber of my being did not want to do it. I look back and wonder why would I do such a thing? Why did I let myself be persuaded by someone else? Why didn't I stand up for myself? Oh, how I wish that I had said, "No." The sin that I committed that day was oral sex. I will never forget the feeling I had that day as I walked away from my boyfriend's car and back into my classroom after lunch break. I felt guilty and I felt very dirty. I felt so sick that I thought that I would actually throw up, right there in the classroom. I told him later that I didn't want to do that anymore, and for a while I didn't. But as I now know, when you continually feed the flesh with passionate lust, you begin to see things differently. The downward spiral of sexual sin had begun in my life and what once sickened me became a routine part of my life.

At the same time these things were occurring, Scott and I attended church services and youth group together, and we both loved the Lord. We would talk about the Lord together as we discussed our future together, already sure that we were going to get married. He was the only boyfriend I had ever had, and I could not imagine my life without him.

Toward the end of my tenth grade year, one afternoon Scott announced to me that he had enlisted in the army. Without ever discussing it with me he signed up for three years in the United States Army. Though I was quite unhappy about it because I knew it meant we would be separated, I loved him so I came to accept it.

Before Scott left for army basic training, we became engaged. Though I was only sixteen, I knew that I wanted to spend the rest of my life with Scott, and he asked my dad for my hand in marriage. Since we had been going out for well over a year, and because my dad knew that I had liked Scott since I was thirteen, I think my dad must have realized that I wasn't going to be talked out of this. From a young age I had demonstrated a consistency about my character and I think that led my dad to believe I was able to make this major decision at age sixteen. So our engagement had the blessings of both sets of parents.

As my friends were switching boyfriends every couple of months, I was getting ready for my fiancé to leave for the army. I felt very sad about this and it seemed like a very difficult time in my life. We were very much in love, and up until this point, Scott and I had not had sexual intercourse. (Or so I thought: As you will read later in this book, oral sex is sexual intercourse, even by the "world's definition.")

As his date of departure approached, we were spending more and more time together. We did not want to leave each other's sides. We laughed together, cried together, and often prayed together. With a diamond on my finger, the man who I loved by my side, and the Lord in our lives, I felt our relationship was all it should be. Early in our relationship Scott and I had pledged that we would never have sex before we were married. We both desired to be virgins when we got married because we wanted to do things God's way and we wanted the Lord to bless our relationship. However, we naively placed ourselves on temptation's path on a regular basis. We had been pushing the boundaries for months, battling the desire to have sexual intercourse. Finally, as the day for him to leave drew near, we no longer resisted.

I will never forget the day that I had sexual intercourse for the first time but unfortunately, it is not a happy memory. (I do not call it "making love" because only a husband and a wife can make love.) I was sixteen years old and I had just committed a sin that I had specifically vowed I would never commit. As a young woman who had a love relationship with my Savior, after I had sexual intercourse, I was distraught. I wept bitterly to my God. I cried to Scott that I never wanted to do that again, until we were married. He felt the same way, and we both repented for the sin that we had just committed. We prayed to the Lord together and asked for forgiveness.

Several weeks later when Scott left for the army, I began to focus more on my relationship with the Lord and I spent a lot of time with my family. While my friends were going out to parties, I was sitting at home with my family. I was a faithful fiancé and I did not even have a desire to party with the others. During high school I never drank alcohol, smoked a cigarette or did any type of drugs. I never even said a curse word nor did I know how to curse. I was considered the good Christian girl to my friends; only *I* knew that I was no longer a virgin. I knew that I had sinned against my precious Savior, and this brought great sadness to my heart. But sadness alone does not turn a sinner from wicked ways. I truly did not want to commit this sin again, but I was not using the right spiritual tools to fight this battle that was within me. During this initial time of separation from Scott I honestly thought that I would not commit this sin again, but I was completely deceived. Though I did not know it at the time, spiritually I was not doing the things that I needed to be doing in order to have victory in this area.

Scott had been in basic training for a couple of months when his parents and I flew to Georgia for his graduation ceremony. Seeing each other again after this first-ever separation was incredible. On the phone, before we met up, he and I discussed and agreed that we were not going to have sex when we saw each other. Regrettably, I learned at age seventeen that "talking the talk" and "walking the walk" are two completely different things.

*He who says he abides in Him ought himself also to walk just as He walked.*
I John 2:6 *(NKJV)*

After Scott's graduation and sharing a meal with his parents we took off in the rental car to spend time together alone; this was our big mistake. We should have stayed in some type of public setting to be together. I'd like to be able to say that we fell into sin, but in fact we *ran* into sin. Despite our pact, again we had sexual intercourse. Only something was different this time: I didn't cry immediately afterwards. I did cry later on, when I flew back to Texas, but while we were together I did not cry at all. I felt some regret, and I knew that I was in sin, but I was not as bothered by it this time.

For the next year and a half Scott and I saw each other about every six months. Each time we saw each other we sinned sexually. Since by now I knew perfectly well this was going to happen each time we were together, I started taking birth control pills. I went to a doctor who prescribed me these pills without my parent's permission and I even stooped to lying to my parents about my whereabouts. I was not yet eighteen, but that didn't matter to the doctor.

The events of my life during this period were illustrating a huge spiritual principle that I was not aware of at the time. As a Christian, when we first step out in sin, we usually feel really bad about it – we often say we feel a sense of conviction. We go before the Lord and tell Him how sorry we are. We often make a multitude of promises to Him, vowing that we will never repeat our sin. But as time passes, if we step out into that sin again, we don't feel quite as bad. And the next time we repeat the sin there is even less regret, and by the next time we don't even know what the big deal is. "Sure, I sinned, but the Lord will forgive me and I will try not to commit this sin again," becomes our attitude. What is taking place is a hardening of the heart. Our hearts are becoming calloused to sin and though we may not acknowledge it, we are slowly beginning to rebel against God.

*"Today, if you will hear His voice, do not harden your hearts as in the rebellion."* Hebrews 3:15b *(NKJ)*

I heard God's voice very loudly the first time that I had pre-marital sexual intercourse, but each time that I committed this sin, I heard Him more faintly. And it was not because He was not speaking to me but because my heart was becoming hard. I didn't want to listen to Him in this area any longer. I became comfortable in my sin. I rationalized that I was going to marry Scott and we were going to spend the rest of our lives together, so what's the big deal? In part the big deal is that one sin will spill over into other areas of a Christian's life. Thinking that I could obey God in other areas of my life, just not *this* area in my life, soon proved to be a lie from the pit of hell. Sin has a domino effect. In a very short time, I became a liar. I was frequently lying to my parents about all kinds of things because of my sexual sin.

So, how was my relationship with the Lord during this time? I still prayed and read a chapter of The Word each day. I attended youth group and church services every week, yet I was in unrepentant sin. It didn't seem that way to me at the time, but looking back, I was just going through the motions. I was so deceived. I thought the Lord and I were okay, other than the fact that I did feel guilty for having sex every six months. I thought the Lord and I had a great relationship together, except for those couple of sins in my life. I was a fornicator and a liar, but other than that, I felt my relationship with the Lord was great. I believed that I was covered in the Lord's grace and I was taking full advantage of that. I was so foolish and deceived. Did I not ever read this verse at age sixteen, seventeen, or eighteen?

*Do you not know that the unrighteous will not inherit the kingdom of God? Do not be deceived. Neither fornicators, nor idolaters, nor adulterers, nor homosexuals, nor sodomites, nor thieves, nor covetous, nor drunkards, nor revilers, nor extortioners will inherit the kingdom of God.* 1 Corinthians 6:9-10 *(NKJV)*

I don't remember seeing it, and if I did, I guess I was just counting on the doctrine of "once saved, always saved" espoused at the Baptist church I attended. The saying goes that "Love is blind" and indeed I really was blind to certain things during this young-and-in-love period of my life. Naturally, Satan liked it that way!

## Marriage

During the time Scott and I were apart, I was easily distracted from the guilt I sometimes felt by the excitement of wedding planning! I had just turned eighteen but I was *so* ready to get married. I longed to become the wife of the man I had loved since I was thirteen. We were married in the Spring at the only time Scott was able to take leave from the Army. Believe it or not, in a period of two short weeks we married, honeymooned, drove to North Carolina, and set up house. Then I flew back to Texas and finished my senior year of high school. People might have guessed, "She must be pregnant," if it hadn't been for the fact that I had been engaged for almost two years.

When it came time to move into our first home together, we found a beautiful apartment which was the ground floor of an enormous two-story home. I loved it from the moment we saw it. As we delightedly moved our belongings in, we noted that both sets of our parents could visit at Christmas because it was so big. We unpacked until the wee hours of the morning and then finally turned in for the night.

As we lay in bed, tired but happy, Scott told me that he was going to have to go away for three weeks for military training and he would also have to do some training on some weekends. It was then, at 18 and living away from my parents for the first time ever, that it dawned on me that I was going to have to stay alone in that huge house! As that realization set in, Scott and I both began feeling very uneasy about living in that home. Out loud Scott prayed, "Lord, if this is not Your will, if You do not want us to stay here, let us know." Suddenly, our bed dropped to the floor! Amazed and alarmed, we immediately got out of bed, packed everything back in the U-haul, and left the house as the sun was just peeking over the horizon. Our landlord was generous enough to return most of our deposit and later that day we found a cozy one-bedroom apartment to be our first home together.

We enjoyed our new married life together immensely. I did get homesick from time to time, but I adjusted well for being so far away from the rest of my family. Scott and I went to church on a regular basis and inside I was relieved that I was no longer plagued by feelings of guilt about our pre-marital sexual relations. As a married woman, I knew I could now enjoy sex with my husband with God's approval. I did regret I had not been a virgin when I married, and I occasionally felt troubled knowing that someday I was going to have to admit that to my children, Oh, if only that had been the only sexual sin that I would have to tell them about. If only my transgressions had ended there!

One Friday evening Scott came home from work with a video for us to watch. Renting movies was big back in the Eighties, and was much cheaper than going to a movie theater. But Scott warned me before he started this movie that it was not our usual fare, but pornography. Shocked and horrified, I told him that we could not watch such a movie—first, because, we were Christians, and second, I believed it was just wrong for any married couple to watch pornography. "Am I not good enough for you?" I pleaded. I was very disturbed and didn't understand why my husband would bring home pornography. Finally I calmed down, and he talked me into watching it, "Just this one time, since it's already been paid for." He told me that if I did not like it we would never have to watch it again. Reluctantly, I watched it with him, and I did not like it at all. I could not fathom how anyone could enjoy watching such movies; to me it was disgusting and nauseating. I told him never, ever to bring pornography into our home again. For a long time, he honored my wishes.

I finished my teen years as a newlywed woman. Even though we are not still married, I have no regrets about marrying at such a young age. I still believe that Scott and I were God's will for one another. I say that because we did join our lives in marriage, and once you *are* married, it is God's will that you stay married. God hates divorce. What God has joined together, let no man put asunder.

However, having lived through all that I will tell you about in this book, I would strongly discourage a couple from getting married if they are in sexual sin. In my opinion, the two in sexual sin should separate because they are not walking in God's will. When you are not in God's will you are not able to make decisions that honor God. In addition, the emotion that is generated by the act of sex outside of marriage, much like a drug, will cloud a person's mind, thus short-circuiting his or her ability to hear God's voice clearly, or even to think logically and realistically about the relationship. Instead of having a *true* (accurate and objective) view of your partner, your feelings will keep you deceived regarding this most-important-of-all human relationships. In effect you will be living a lie. If you think you are truly in love and that God would bless your marriage, then you should separate for a while and be reunited in God's timing. It's very important to walk in purity for months before you marry. Walking in purity demonstrates so many things in your relationship with the Lord, and it proves your character both to yourself and your future spouse. I will go into depth concerning those thoughts later on in this book.

You may be thinking, "Who are you, Stacey, to be preaching about walking in purity?" As I continue to share my story you will understand how I can speak about purity. You will understand why walking in purity is a very strong passion of mine. Purity is a gift from the Lord that He gives to each one of us. It's our choice as to whether or not we walk in purity during our singleness, in our dating days, and in our marriage. Purity is the key to the mind. As my pastor exhorts, "Battles are won or lost in the mind." Evil and purity cannot exist together.

At age thirteen I was very pure, but evil began to creep into my life throughout my teen years. I did not stand in victory over the sexual sin that was in my life. The enemy saw my weakness and the enemy knew that I was not using the right tools for this type of battle. Initially, before engaging in each sin, I wrestled against participating in each one of them. But I did not stand strong in my convictions, or in my faith. Succumbing to sinful actions became a pattern in my life, a very bad pattern, which destroyed the pure heart of the girl I had been, the girl who truly loved the Lord and sought always to please him, who cried in her daddy's arms when she knew she had fallen short.

*Beware, brethren, lest there be in any of you an evil heart of unbelief in departing from the living God; but exhort one another daily, while it is called "Today," lest any of you be hardened through the deceitfulness of sin.* Hebrews 3:12-13 *(NKJV)*

May I encourage you, *fall more in love with Jesus TODAY!*

# ✝
# TWO
# The Downward Spiral of Sin

Scott and I started our family with the birth of twin girls when I was twenty. Four years later we had another little girl. We spent time with our girls and our extended family; life was full and we were happy. At the church we attended on a regular basis we completed an evening parenting class over several months. Of course we had our ups and downs; at times we had plenty of money, and at other times we were scraping pennies together to buy a gallon of milk. Our spiritual lives, our emotional relationship and our physical relationship with one another all seemed good. "Seemed" is the critical word. Things began to change around the time I was twenty-five.

## Dangerous Games

For seven years the sexual relationship we enjoyed as a married couple was very normal and satisfying I believed. But apparently something was going on with Scott that I didn't know about until Scott started asking me questions that made me feel uncomfortable. He wanted to know if I found other men attractive. For months I kept answering this question, "No," but he persistently quizzed me on this again and again. "There's no way in this world that you don't find any other man besides me attractive," he would insist, and, "It's perfectly normal to find other people attractive, Stacey." He pressed me to know *who* in my life, besides him, I found attractive. I argued that we were Christians and we should not engage in such discussions. Sharing such fantasies would be fun for us, he countered. "It's normal for married couples to have fantasies together," he argued. Firmly I continued to resist him on this, refusing to play his fantasy game.

13

For months, off and on, Scott kept at me about this. One weekend we were staying in a hotel for an out-of-town wedding and again he initiated this line of conversation. By this time I was very upset and even angry about it; I just didn't understand why he wouldn't stop as I had begged him to do. I will never forget that evening. In my anger I did something that I did not want to do. He had worn me down and I thought if I cooperated with his game just this one time then he would stop hounding me to do this. I gave in--I gave him the name of someone we knew, and he created a fantasy. Though I had hoped that my playing along would put an end to such conversations, in fact it did exactly the opposite. That night, in our marriage bed, that little puppy of sin that I told you about was birthed.

Every wife wants to please her husband, and I was no different. I didn't understand why Scott liked this game, but I could see that it pleased him and after doing it a few times, it didn't bother me as much. I never imagined that this was going to give Satan a foothold in our lives. Making up fantasies became a routine part of our marriage bed. Thus the downward spiral of sexual sin within my marriage began. I would question him from time to time about whether this was really OK for us as Christians, but he continued to reassure me that "the marriage bed is undefiled." As he interpreted this scripture, whatever we as a married couple wanted to do together was not sin. Here's the scripture that he used:

*Marriage is honorable among all, and the bed undefiled; but fornicators and adulterers God will judge.* Hebrews 13:4 *(NKJV)*

But having lived through this experience, and knowing what it led us to do, I am as certain as I can be that these fantasies *are* sin, even in the marriage bed. I was naïve and immature in the Lord at that time. My husband had quoted the New King James Version of that scripture, and had interpreted it wrongly. The meaning is clearer in the New International Version:

*Marriage should be honored by all, and <u>the marriage bed kept pure</u>, for God will judge the adulterer and <u>all the sexually immoral</u>.* Hebrews 13:4 *(NIV)*

Perhaps you, like others with whom I have shared my story, find it rather unbelievable that a married couple can have sinful sex. Perhaps you can't imagine what in the world I could be talking about. Stay with me as I explain how it is possible that a married couple can have impure sex. My story is a testimony to that. The sex that my husband and I began to have was sexually immoral. Urgently I am warning any of you who may be playing these fantasy games with your husband, thinking that it's no big deal. As my story continues, you will see just how treacherous this path really is. Stop the fantasies now! Stop playing around with this type of sin. It will destroy your marriage and it will destroy you. I know too well that this type of sin will turn you into someone you never, ever want to become.

As I continue to narrate the downward spiral of sexual sin in my life, it will be easy for you to think, "I would never do that." I expect you to think that way because I had the same thoughts when I was first urged to do these things. I vowed I would *never* do the things that I ended up doing. We are mortal creatures and we all find that as we feed our flesh, it gets stronger and our principles get weaker. Committing a sin again and again drags you into other sins and those lead, ultimately to a nose dive. A crash is inevitable, if you do not let Jesus Christ intervene.

I know that I am forgiven. I know I am no longer the woman controlled by sexual sin that I once was. I know I am a new creation in Christ. But *you* don't know who I am now; you don't really know me at all. I hope you are getting to know me through reading my story. More important, and the purpose for this book, I want you to get to know The Deliverer, possibly in a way that you have never seen Him before. I want you to see Him in action, in one woman's life.

Evil is darkness. Evil is sadness. Evil is emptiness. As you read the words that I have written, it should affect you. God wants you to be disturbed by the sin that took place in my life. If my testimony evokes no emotion in you, then something is not right in your heart. Our hearts should feel broken over the sins of others in the world, and if they are not, then we need to ask the Lord to give us His heart for others. If you see or hear of the sin in others' lives and merely judge them, having no compassion for them, then please ask the Lord to give you His heart for sinners.

*"Judge not, that you be not judged. For with what judgment you judge, you will be judged; and with the measure you use, it will be measured back to you.*

15

*And why do you look at the speck in your brother's eye, but do not consider the plank in your own eye? Or how can you say to your brother, 'Let me remove the speck from your eye'; and look, a plank is in your own eye? Hypocrite! First remove the plank from your own eye, and then you will see clearly to remove the speck out of your brother's eye.* Matthew 7:1-5 *(NKJV)*

I am sharing with you the details of the journey in sexual sin that I traveled in my marriage *hoping* that you will never take that path. From the depth of my soul, I shout to you, "Beware! Turn around! Do not take the wide path that this world offers. Only danger is ahead if you refuse to turn around."

*Enter by the narrow gate; for wide is the gate and broad is the way that leads to destruction, and there are many who go in by it. Because narrow is the gate and difficult is the way which leads to life, and there are few who find it.* Matthew 7:13-14 *(NKJV)*

Unfortunately, I have learned a lot about sin. It is an unusual creature. Sin may start off as a cute little puppy which you think you can control with a cage and a leash, but that cute little puppy is a disguise from the enemy. When you continue to feed that cute little puppy it will grow up to be more like a ferocious wolf. When grown, you won't be able to keep it hidden or manage it. Instead, it will have you in bondage.

*"But if you do not do so, then take note, you have sinned against the LORD; and be sure your sin will find you out.* Numbers 32:23 *(NKJV)*

*Be sober, be vigilant; because your adversary the devil walks about like a roaring lion, seeking whom he may devour.* 1 Peter 5:8 *(NKJV)*

As I was jogging this morning (I am a runner) I was talking with the Lord about how I am to continue writing this book. Begging Him for wisdom, I cried, "Lord, this book is going to be filled with sin. It is not a pretty story at all. But I know, without a doubt, that you told me to include the *details* of my story. How will the readers be able to bear hearing about all this evil before they get to the beautiful part where you rescued and delivered me?"

And of course, He answered me! He will always give us our answer when we wait patiently for it. He guided me on how to structure this book. As we retrace the steps through the muck and mire of my journey into sexual sin and then beyond, to my glorious freedom from that sin, we will stop for needed refreshment along the way. At certain points I will share about the magnificent things of the Lord, using incidents from my past and recent life in which God revealed his abundant goodness to me. He has done some amazing, crazy things in my life these past seventeen years since I rededicated my life to Him--things that will make you smile, laugh and perhaps even cry, because of God's goodness; and things that will fill your heart with joy and excitement.

Though we will travel together along the evil trail that took me to the edge of hell, I will also show you my current route--the holy path that has taken me into the presence of Almighty God. He is my best friend and He blows my mind all of the time! He is the most real person to me in my entire life. I am going to share with you who He is to me now and who He has been to me since I returned to Him. In this way, I pray my testimony will reassure and encourage you, and perhaps inspire *you* to the intimacy I share with my Savior.

*Then I heard a loud voice saying in heaven, "Now salvation, and strength, and the kingdom of our God, and the power of His Christ have come, for the accuser of our brethren, who accused them before our God day and night, has been cast down. "And <u>they overcame him by the blood of the Lamb and by the word of their testimony</u>, and they did not love their lives to the death. "Therefore rejoice, O heavens, and you who dwell in them! Woe to the inhabitants of the earth and the sea! For the devil has come down to you, having great wrath, because he knows that he has a short time."* Revelation 12:10-12 *(NKJV)*

## DECEPTIVE DEVICES

Let me share some incredible news with you. As my pastor proclaims frequently, "We win! Read the back of the book! We win!" The victory has already been won, the price already paid. Jesus said from the cross, *"It is finished!" And bowing His head, He gave up His spirit.* John 19:30b *(NKJV)*

The enemy may be messing around in your head; he may be shooting those fiery darts into your brain, giving you sinful thoughts, but that he has already lost the war is certain. He will attack you fiercely, because

17

he knows his time is short. It's already finished for him; it's just a matter of time before he is cast into the lake of fire eternally.

*The devil, who deceived them, was cast into the lake of fire and brimstone where the beast and the false prophet are. And they will be tormented day and night forever and ever.* Revelation 20:10 *(NKJV)*

The devil is the great deceiver and he continued to deceive me. As I had mentioned before, fantasies became a part of my marriage bed. For months Scott and I included fantasies in our sex life. I had accepted this to please my husband, but as you may know, sin always grows when you continue to feed it. One day Scott brought home a device that the world calls a sex toy. I do not like to refer to such devices as toys because calling them toys makes them sound innocent and harmless, yet that could not be further from the truth. At the time I think I had heard about these things but I had never seen one. At first I started laughing, saying, "Now what is that? What are you supposed to do with it? That's sick." I still had an innocence about me that just couldn't understand the ways of this world. And once again, I protested, "We are Christians. We can't do this." It just didn't seem right to me, or normal; I didn't feel right in my spirit about using such a device. I resisted for quite a while, but my husband kept telling me it would be fine and I eventually gave in, thinking, "What could be the harm? My husband wants me to, so how could this be wrong?" Using these devices now became a part of our marriage bed, and a part of my life. Thus I continued along the downward spiral of sexual sin; what once I refused to do, I now began to do on a regular basis.

Perhaps you are messing around with these devices with your spouse, or you're using them as a single person. Maybe you think using these devices is no big deal at all. But let me explain to you why it *is* a big deal. Please heed me on this because I know that the Lord has given me wisdom concerning these deceptive devices. They were created by the world and in the enemy's hands they will be used to destroy you because they destroy the beautiful, intimate sexual activities that our Lord designed and blesses. I know what I am talking about because these deceptive devices became a huge part of my life. I ended up with a box full of them, which I once threw across the room at my husband when I was in complete sexual bondage.

The Lord created man and woman for one another. The husband's body belongs to the wife and the wife's body belongs to the husband.

*The husband should fulfill his marital duty to his wife, and likewise the wife to her husband. The wife's body does not belong to her alone but also to her husband. In the same way, the husband's body does not belong to him alone but also to his wife.* 1 Corinthians 7:3-4 *(NIV)*

The Lord designed marriage and the marriage bed. He created our bodies in such a way that a husband and wife can please one another sexually. Our bodies were made for one another. Nowhere in scripture do we see that God created other objects for sexual pleasure. Read the Song of Solomon; it is the sex manual God gave his people, and it alludes to an array of sexual activities for a husband and wife to enjoy. But nowhere in scripture is there even a suggestion that anything more than the bodies of the man and woman is needed for sexual pleasure.

I realize that the thoughts I present in this book may seem scandalous to some Christians, but that should not be. The mass media shout at us about "Sex" wherever we go. Our schools insist on teaching our children about sex. Our teens are not only talking about sex all of the time among themselves but far too frequently they are experimenting with sex, too. College students are consumed with sex. Movies, magazines and television portray average women in their thirties and forties eagerly seeking ways to spice up their sex lives. Yet most of the time, most churches respond, "Hush now. We can't speak of such a thing. We must keep that to ourselves."

But the church mustn't remain so tight-lipped about sex. This book is an attempt to break the silence that the church has maintained throughout the Sexual Revolution that began almost fifty years ago. Believers need the church to speak out about sex to provide correct Biblical teaching on the subject. Why do I believe that? Because as a Christian girl who knew very little about sex I was an easy target for the enemy. I had no idea that there could be any danger in the sexual activities that took place in a marriage bed. I never would have imagined that the sexual relationship between a husband and a wife could be the thing that would bring that marriage to total destruction and divorce. And if this could happen easily in a Christian marriage, my dear friend, what about our lost and dying world that is drenched in the sexual realm? Just look around: Sexual sin is on the rise in every arena.

We, as Christians, can no longer be silent about these things. Sexual bondage is a very real and powerful stronghold. Those who are just beginning to dabble in sexual sin must be warned of the danger that lies ahead of them. Sexual bondage is hard to escape. Those trapped in it must know that there is hope, that there is a way out. Only we Christians are equipped to teach them that Jesus Christ can set them free, and that once they are free, they will be free indeed. We must assure them that God gives His complete forgiveness and His abundant, healing love. They need to know, and we must tell them.

*For "whoever calls on the name of the Lord shall be saved." How then shall they call on Him in whom they have not believed? And how shall they believe in Him of whom they have not heard? And how shall they hear without a preacher? And how shall they preach unless they are sent? As it is written: "How beautiful are the feet of those who preach the gospel of peace, who bring glad tidings of good things!" Romans 10:13-15 (NKJV)*

## Defiling Ourselves

In my marriage we progressed from creating fantasies to using sexual devices. Of course when I speak of these devices you know they are used for a specific sexual act. I know you are thinking, "She's not really going to say it, is she?" Yes, I am going to say the "M" word, masturbation. And why shouldn't I say it, since in the check-out line at the grocery store the headline on a magazine cover screams to me, "Seven Ways to Masturbate." The world has taken something very beautiful that the Lord created for married people and has turned it into a game for everyone to play, with anyone, anytime, anywhere! I've noticed that you can even buy a sexual device at your local pharmacy; that, to me, is crazy! And on television channels that are *not* x-rated you will hear advertisements for these devices—these tools of the enemy.

In my opinion, masturbation is a sin. I believe that scripture supports that opinion. I realize that even some well-known and highly esteemed Christian psychologists purport that masturbation is not a sin. They claim it is a normal part of being human. I believe many Christians are doing it, but not admitting it. I have a lot of grace for women struggling in this area, and I understand if you totally disagree with me. But if you think that masturbation is not a sin, I have one thing to ask of you. Please go to the Lord in prayer concerning this; seek Him and study His Word to know His answer.

I prefer to use the term self-sex instead of masturbation. My pastor in Ft. Lauderdale spoke of self-sex from the pulpit, which blew me away the first time I heard him preach about it, declaring that it is a sin. All sex outside of marriage is a sin, and self-sex is sex. Towards the end of this book I will cite scripture and explain more about what the Lord has taught me concerning self-sex. For now, if you do not agree with my assessment, please seek the Lord yourself concerning self-sex. I myself saw nothing at all wrong with it, until it controlled me. Once I came to be in bondage to masturbation, I wanted to stop but I just couldn't, no matter what I tried. Consider this: Why does a person masturbate? I know you are thinking, "She's not really going to say it, is she?" Yes, I am going to say the "O" word, orgasm. A person masturbates in order to have an orgasm. A person masturbates so that the "flesh" can feel really good. So self-sex is clearly feeding our flesh, and our flesh is lusting.

*For all that is in the world-- the lust of the flesh, the lust of the eyes, and the pride of life-- is not of the Father but is of the world.* I John 2:16 *(NKJV)*

I believe it's time for an amazing God story. Let's take a breather from the downward spiral of sexual sin; I will tell you a story that will make you smile and feel uplifted. God is so good!

## Joy in Trials

In April of 2010, the Lord called me to a much higher level of faith in my life. In order for me to answer this call, a lot of things in my life had to change. I had to increase my faith in the Lord, and the only way to do that was to spend more time with Him; in His Word, in prayer, in worshipping, in running (more about that one later) and also by fasting. I had fasted in the past, but I had never fasted routinely. Now, since this experience in my life, I fast in a variety of ways on a regular basis.

In January 2011, I did my first juice fast. I drank only juice during the fast, except that because I am a runner I also drank one protein shake a day. I had decided to fast for twenty-one days, and when I later discovered that Daniel the Prophet had fasted for twenty-one days I was excited knowing that I had chosen the same timeframe as he. This fast was the hardest I have ever done, but was also an incredible experience.

I viewed the juice fast as a new adventure for the Lord and I to take together. I knew that He would speak to me during this fast, which He did, but He did so in a very subtle way. Because I was not eating food at all and only drinking juice and protein, I think I expected something huge to happen. But as each day passed, nothing huge happened. Or at least that is what my human mind thought. I had no idea about what the Lord was up to but I realized later that He was working on me in ways that I could not see with my human eyes.

Actually, the Lord did give me something huge to do, though it didn't seem huge at the time. He directed me to write down my story, or testimony; but I didn't realize that He had plans to have my story published for the whole world to read. It was in January 2011 that He first told me to write my story, but I didn't put feet to my faith until the end of August of that year. It was then that I began writing down what you are now holding in your hands.

On the day that my fast was to end I was scheduled to attend a prayer meeting so I planned that I would break my fast right after my prayer group, with some raisin bread that I took along with me. As it happened, I felt led by the Lord to use the raisin bread for our group to have communion. I had not planned on doing that, but the Lord had; He even brought my pastor to that prayer meeting unexpectedly so I got to share my bread with him and the other women.

At home a few hours later I ate about six bites of pasta and felt full. Then it all began, what God had been silently preparing me for during the fast: a myriad of trials started to come my way. First, I had a tire blow out when I was driving just a few miles from my home. A few days later the transmission in my car broke and the mechanic estimated repairs would cost $2,900, which we did not have. Next, after a few more days, we were denied a refinancing mortgage on our home. And soon after that all the water pipes, and I mean ALL the pipes, in our home froze. That repair was expected to run $2,700, which we did not have. Shortly after that event I had two more tires blow out (yes, that's three blow outs in about three weeks) while I was driving my husband's car. And finally, on top of those mundane difficulties, my husband's chronic illness of fourteen years began to increase in severity.

"Okay, so where is the amazing, uplifting God story?" you are wondering. What is amazing is that through all of these troubles I did not shed one tear. I did not become angry, upset or even feel stressed. Perhaps you think, "Now that's just not normal." You are right that it's not normal; it is *supernatural* that the Lord caused me to truly rejoice in my trials. With each difficulty, I had more of His joy! It made no sense at all. I felt like a volcano erupting, a Holy Ghost volcano! I was exploding with Holy Ghost lava on all of those around me.

During that time period I could not stop smiling, laughing, praising, and worshipping the Lord. My daughter and I washed the dishes, as well as our clothing, outside in the horse trough, all the while singing songs of praise. We knew it was crazy, absolutely crazy. I call it 'Crazy God'! The Lord knew ahead of time what was going to happen in my life and graciously prepared me. His timing is perfect and it was no accident that I fasted when I did. The Lord gave me supernatural strength from my time of fasting, and He poured it out on me during that time of trials.

At our church's midweek service I was even able to publicly exhort my fellow parishioners, saying, "We mustn't focus on our circumstances, but instead keep our attention on the Lord." I encouraged them that no matter what difficulties we are going through, Jesus Christ is enough. He and He alone should be enough for us. He should be the One who satisfies us completely.

*For He satisfies the longing soul, and fills the hungry soul with goodness.* Psalms 107:9 *(NKJV)*

It was on Tuesday night that I gave that testimony at church. Two days later that incredible God who we serve showed up in an amazing way. I have never seen money grow on trees, but I have now seen a van fall from Heaven! A man who my family does not know, who lives three and a half hours away from us, gave us a minivan! Somehow he had heard about our family, about all of the trials that we were going through and about our faith in Jesus Christ. He wanted to bless us.

As I type this page, I can see out my window right now my "Heavenly Van," which is what I call it. I also see my broken down Monte Carlo on the right side of our yard, still waiting for that transmission to fall from Heaven.

So, my dear friend, be assured that God is so good, so faithful and so real. He watches over His children all of the time. It would have been okay if He had not given me that van. When the circumstances all around me were a mess I was not a mess, because of Him. That I was filled with His peace and His joy during those trying weeks, that is the amazing God story! The van was just the cherry on top for me.

*Then I will go to the altar of God, to God my exceeding joy; and on the harp I will praise You, O God, my God.* Psalms 43:4 *(NKJV)*

## THE DOOR TO ADDICTION

By the time I was twenty-six, the Lord had blessed us with another baby. I had been married for eight years and was now the mother of 4 girls. Scott's job took him out of town for months at a time but usually he would be able to return home for at least one weekend each month. Though I went to church with the girls almost every Sunday when he was away, we did not attend regularly when Scott was at home. It was during this period that Scott brought home pornographic movies again. This time, I was in a much different place spiritually than I had been when I was eighteen. I still didn't understand how anyone could enjoy watching such films, and again I told my husband that I thought to do so was sin. As previously, he assured me that if we, as a married couple, were okay with it, then it was not a sin. And even though I did not really believe that as I watched, I was tired of fighting with my husband about all of these sexual issues. When I asked myself what I should do, as a woman and as his wife, I reflected on these facts: I had known him since I was thirteen. He was the only boyfriend that I ever had and the only man I had ever kissed. We had been married for eight years and had four children together. I missed him when he was away. So what should I do?

Not having any idea about the danger and evil involved in these behaviors, I did the worst thing that I could have possibly done. I did as my husband requested and began to watch pornography with him.

That little puppy that I told you about was growing. I'm sure the enemy was very pleased with what was taking place in my marriage. He was roaming all around my house, and, though I was completely unaware of it, he was taking over my marriage bed in a very seductive way.

Even after all of these years, as I am typing this, the tears are streaming down my face. Not because I feel guilty, or condemned, but because I was tricked and deceived. I never would have imagined that sex between a husband and a wife could become impure and ungodly. My innocence was lost completely as pornography began to take over my mind. It took months of watching it with my husband before I enjoyed it, but the day did come when I, too, delighted in watching pornography. It is still unfathomable to me, but that is exactly what took place.

We, being modern and sophisticated, naively believe that what we put into our minds will not hurt us. We think that what we listen to and allow our ears to hear will not affect us. We trust that what our eyes see will not change us. We believe those things, my dear friends, because we consider them with a human mind. But if we contemplate them in the spiritual realm, we will see clearly, and we will think differently concerning these things. We must acknowledge that there are ramifications of feeding our flesh, and then we will realize that what we place in front of our eyes can certainly change us; what we hear can profoundly affect us; and that the thoughts that enter our minds can deeply hurt us.

At the onset of participating in an addictive sin, such as sex-outside-of-marriage, use of illicit drugs, or abuse of alcohol, a person usually experiences no negative consequences. In fact, he (or she) is probably really enjoying the sin that is being committed; there is a sense of pleasure, even excitement, and no harm is apparent. But the Bible (Hebrews 25b) even tells us that the pleasures of sins are passing. We enjoy our new sin at first, but over time, we become bored with it and that particular sin no longer arouses our flesh as it did in the beginning. We have to add to that first sin. For example, marijuana use can often lead to cocaine use, and then to heroin. In my case, the use of fantasies led us to use sexual devices and self-sex, and then to pornography. It's the downward spiral of sin. And as the sin grows, one's heart begins to change: it begins to become hardened towards sin. The one sinning no longer feels any guilt or regret; the sin no longer seems so bad. As one gets used to sinning, it doesn't even seem like sin anymore.

Remember what I said to my husband when I was eighteen? "No way, buddy, are you ever bringing pornography into our home again!" So what happened? Why did I allow it in at age twenty-six? Because the things I had permitted to enter my ears, eyes and mind during the ensuing years had changed me; I had come to think of sex in a much different way because of the fantasies and the sexual devices, and my heart was changing, one beat at a time. So when pornography came knocking at my door at this stage, I was a much different person. I reluctantly let it in, but I did open the door because it was no longer a stranger to me.

Consider this: How do you become friends with someone you don't know? First, you are introduced to him; then you spend time with him. Getting to know him by letting your guard down and becoming comfortable with him, you begin to build that friendship. Gradually, you become good friends. Sin befriends us in the same way. I was introduced to sexual sin. I spent time in sexual sin. I was getting to know it and I was becoming comfortable with it. Sexual sin was becoming my friend.

Pornography is a crazy thing. Medical experts have actually proven that there is a chemical reaction that takes place in the human brain while the person is being aroused by pornography; this is why it is addictive. Let me be clear: it is addictive, but it is not a disease. The world has taken so many addictive sins and labeled them with the word "disease." Sin is sin, let's at least admit it.

But how could I begin to enjoy pornography? How could I, as a woman, appreciate such a thing? As I said, I started spending time with it, and gradually it was becoming my friend. Scott and I had been verbalizing fantasies for about a year, so now, with the pornographic movies, we were *watching* fantasies. It was not that great a leap. You see, what is portrayed in pornography is not real, it *is* a fantasy. Instead of imagining people, we were now watching people on the screen. I only viewed the movies with my husband, and typically use of pornography involves at least three senses because you are watching something with your eyes, hearing it with your ears, and at the same time your body is actively engaged in the experience. This is why the use of pornography is very dangerous. While this activity was happening in our bedroom, in the spiritual world a demonic pep rally was taking place. What I mean is that Satan and his demons were cheering for this game of sex that would destroy real love and my marriage. Pornography is a game, but it's not a pretend game; it's a game that can destroy your life. For the moment you may feel like a winner, but you will lose, and you will lose enormously if you do not stop.

Through use of pornography in our marriage bed I was filling my mind with sexual immorality. I was seeing it right in front of my eyes. I was hearing it, and my flesh was being fed with more intensity than it ever had been before because of the multiple layers of input. Pornography gave my flesh a high that it had never experienced. Since I had never used drugs and at this point in my life had never even taken a sip of alcohol I cannot compare the experience I was having with those things. But I can tell you that the physical relationship I was sharing with my husband was *out of this world*. Indeed, it was other-worldly, and I had no idea about how evil this other world was. This very dark world that I was becoming a part of, one sin at a time, I have come to recognize as the downward spiral of sexual sin. It was taking place in and taking over my life; again, what once I had refused to do, I now began to do routinely.

Recently I was telling a friend of mine at work about this part of my testimony. She remarked, "I guess you watched the pornography with him because you were afraid otherwise he would have sex with someone else." Here's the crazy thing: I wasn't afraid of that at all. There was just something about me that was so trusting when it came to my husband. I trusted Scott with my life. I thought he was crazy in love with me, that he would never ever lie to me. I thought I meant the world to him. It never entered my mind that he would betray my trust. I know how incredibly foolish that sounds, looking at this picture that I have painted for you, but I am being honest. Truly, I still trusted him. I suppose because he was my first love and my only love, and because I felt that he treated me like a precious treasure. I thought we were so very much in love. But if I was not afraid of losing him, then why did I watch the pornography with him when I didn't approve of it? Because I loved him and wanted to please him.

I know there are a lot of women who, because of their love for their husbands, are doing things that they do not want to do. I thought I knew the character and actions of love, and you may think that you know that too. True love, Godly love, will never ask you to do something sinful. (1 Corinthians 13:4-7) I didn't stand up to my husband. I could not come up against him because I, as his wife, was the weaker vessel. I was not able to stand up against my husband but I should have been strong enough to stand up for my God. Each wife is supposed to submit to our own husband but we are never obliged to submit to him if he is leading us into sin. If I had been standing strong for the Lord, then I would have been strong enough to stand up to my husband concerning sexual sin. I gave into sin because I let go of my God.

Let's take a breather and let me tell you a life-changing God story!

# The Lost Keys

I had recently rededicated my life to the Lord and was living in Ft. Lauderdale, Florida. At the time, Scott and I were separating, and probably going to divorce. I realize I am jumping ahead in my story before we get to that place in my testimony, but you can already tell that my marriage was headed in that direction.

I decided to move back to Texas because I didn't know anyone in Florida. Though I had started attending a Calvary Chapel I had not made any friends yet. My parents wanted me to move back to Texas so they would be able to provide the help and emotional support I was going to need as a newly-single mom of four little girls. Aware that my twins had been chronic asthmatics since they were two years old, my parents understood that a great deal of extra work and care were required. Moving back to Texas seemed like the logical thing to do, but I was vaguely sensing the Lord telling me to stay in Florida. Having newly rededicated my life to Him, I was not *certain* of the Lord's voice. And it just didn't make sense to me to stay in Florida with no friends or family to help me. So, ignoring that feeling deep within which urged me to stay, I decided to move back to Texas.

I packed up the car, loaded the girls in, and we hit the road for Texas. My parents had agreed to drive from Texas to meet me that evening at a hotel midway along my journey. After about four hours we stopped at a huge gas station/rest stop. I led my little darlings into the restroom, bought them some snacks, and then returned to the car. But there was a problem: I could not find the keys anywhere. Even though my testimony may make you doubt it, I am a very responsible person. I had never, ever lost my keys before in all my life. I remembered placing my keys in my purse after getting out of the car, but they were not there. Though I searched and retraced my steps, they were not anywhere! Confused and upset, I reported the keys missing to the management office of this rest stop; then the girls and I just sat there, for what turned out to be hours. Finally, as I sat there, I prayed.

Since rededicating my life to the Lord, I knew God's hand was upon me once again, and that He was beginning to work in my life in a much different way than He ever had before. I was sensing His very presence in my life in an almost tangible way. There at the rest stop, I was certain that He had a plan and a purpose for me and for my girls. I recognized that He had not abandoned me in my sin, and I began to discern what He was telling me, which was to stay in Florida. That made no sense at all to my human mind. I was sure that Scott and I were not getting back together and I truly had no one I knew to help me with my young daughters. I cried out to God that I just didn't understand. "Why don't You want me to go back home to Texas to be with my family?" Not understanding, but sure of God's leading, there at the rest stop far from home I made the decision to follow the Lord no matter what. And no matter what happened, I would trust Him.

With that decision made and now at peace, I looked up to find the rest stop manager handing me my keys. He said that someone had brought them to his desk saying, "These keys belong to that young woman with four little girls," and then had simply walked away. I am not sure how the Lord orchestrated this event. I mean, was that person an angel? Was he just another Christian who found my keys somewhere and was given a word of knowledge? Was it the Lord Himself who returned the keys? The details of how it happened don't matter to me but I am absolutely sure that the Lord took my keys from me, and then returned them after I made the decision to listen to Him, no matter what.

Since my parents were already traveling to meet us and we had no cell phones, I quickly loaded up the girls and we returned to Ft. Lauderdale. That evening I called my parents at the hotel where we were supposed to meet and I told them what had happened. I explained how the Lord was working in my life and that I was not going to be moving back to Texas. As you can imagine; they were not happy with my decision at all; in fact, they were very upset with me and I could understand that. Over the phone I shared with them some of the events that had taken place in my marriage so that they could see that I was a very troubled woman. They loved me and their granddaughters dearly and they sincerely wanted to help. Knowing I had no friends in Florida, they were very worried about us. Though they urged and pleaded with me to start out again for Texas the next day, I refused. I had to listen to the Lord, I told them firmly.

About a week later, feeling intensely pressured to move back to Texas by my loving and concerned parents, brother, and sisters, I began to question God. I talked to Him a lot, and I pleaded that I was just not strong enough to stay in Florida by myself. I expressed to Him that I was sorry but that I really needed to be with my family. Since I knew that He would still be with me in Texas and that He would forgive me for not staying in Florida all by myself with four little girls, I again made the decision, on a Saturday afternoon, to move back to Texas. With that settled in my mind, I gathered the girls and headed for my church's Saturday evening service.

I could hardly believe what God did next. Pastor Bob's teaching that night was on this scripture from Genesis: *Now the LORD had said to Abram: "Get out of your country, from your family and from your father's house, to a land that I will show you."* Genesis 12:1 (NKJV)

And then Pastor Bob announced from the pulpit, "I was not planning to teach this scripture this evening but the Lord directed me to say *this* to someone very specifically. Your family is pressuring you to come home but the Lord has told you to trust Him and to go where He is telling you to go. Never do anything because your family is pressuring you. Always do what you know the Lord is telling you to do. He will bless you for it.'"

I could not believe my ears! "Can this be real?" I thought. In shock, yet with awe and thankfulness, I realized that this was a personal message from God to me. At the time, Pastor Bob knew nothing about me or my circumstances, and there were five thousand people who attended this church. Did God really care so much for me? *Now* I surely knew the answer to that was "Yes! He really *is* concerned about me personally and specifically." Maybe that word was also for someone else who was there that night, but it was definitely for me, and I knew it with all my heart. I left the service that night radically changed: I had a whole new mindset about God that I continue to have to this very day.

Later that evening as I sat in my backyard hammock, looking up at the sky, I asked the Lord to please give me the strength to tell my family my final decision. I promised I was not going to change my mind again. I was still a bit frightened and I cried to the Lord that I just did not understand but that I was going to try very hard to trust Him on this. For the first time ever I heard Him speak directly to me, not audibly with my ears, but spiritually. In my heart and in my mind, I heard Him say so very clearly, "Do not go to the left or to the right. Keep your eyes on Me, Stacey, and everything will be okay."

For the second time that day I was awestruck. "I heard God!" I thought. "The God of the universe spoke and He spoke to me directly!" Shocked, yet amazed and excited, I realized He is real and He is with me. Although He knew everything that I had done, He was still talking to me. At the time, I had no idea that the words He spoke to me were actually in His Word--not the exact words, but very close. He was telling me to stay in Florida and to continue to attend Calvary Chapel. There I was being taught The Word, verse by verse, and my life was changing rapidly and dramatically for the Lord.

*"Only be strong and very courageous, that you may observe to do according to all the law which Moses My servant commanded you; <u>do not turn from it to the right hand or to the left</u>, that you may prosper wherever you go. "This Book of the Law shall not depart from your mouth, but you shall meditate in it day and night, that you may observe to do according to all that is written in it. For then you will make your way prosperous, and then you will have good success. "Have I not commanded you? Be strong and of good courage; do not be afraid, nor be dismayed, for the LORD your God is with you wherever you go." Joshua 1:7-9 (NKJV)*

Now you know why it is with such great confidence that I assure you that God speaks to His children. The question is, are His children listening? During this major transition in my life I was blessed to be learning what I most needed to know--how to hear the still small voice of the Lord. What I learned in the months (and years) that followed was that the more I listened and the more I stepped out in faith and obedience, the more He spoke to me. It was incredible! More important, *He* is incredible!

*Then He said, "Go out, and stand on the mountain before the LORD." And behold, the LORD passed by, and a great and strong wind tore into the mountains and broke the rocks in pieces before the LORD, but the LORD was not in the wind; and after the wind an earthquake, but the LORD was not in the earthquake; and after the earthquake a fire, but the LORD was not in the fire; and after the fire a still small voice. So it was, when Elijah heard it, that he wrapped his face in his mantle and went out and stood in the entrance of the cave. Suddenly a voice came to him, and said, "What are you doing here, Elijah?"* I Kings 19:11-13 *(NKJV)*

Since that day God spoke to me in the hammock, I have never turned back. I trust my Heavenly Father completely. I may not always understand His ways or reasons, but I know I don't need to understand, I just have to trust. The Lord had a very specific reason He wanted me to stay in Florida. As I would later know, it was because He wanted me to experience what true love is. He wanted to show me how I, as a daughter of the King, should be treated.

# THREE
## Bondage Begins

Before continuing with the story into my season of depravity, I would like to share a few things with you. Remember that the Lord directed me to include "details" in the writing of my testimony, and He used the story of the woman at the well in John 4 and the story of David and Bathsheba in II Samuel 11. My story leads deeper into darkness, and you may not understand why I continue to share these details of my sexual sin. Perhaps you think, "Hasn't she shared enough already?" I don't *enjoy* telling the story, but after you have read my whole story, I believe you will understand that if I stopped here I would not have given you a complete and clear picture of just how low the downward spiral of sin can lead you. I have not yet expressed to you the real dangers and depth of sexual sin. It can go very, very deep.

## A Primer on Sin

You could say that sin goes to the very depth of the earth. Sin comes straight from the evil source, and that source is the depths of hell. The enemy is not satisfied to get his hooks into you, or to bite you with his sharp teeth and draw some blood; no, he wants to totally and completely devour you. The *Merriam-Webster's 11th Collegiate Dictionary* definition of devour is, "to eat up greedily or ravenously," and the example used is that of lions devouring their prey.

Sin definitely arises from the deeds of the evil one, but sin also emanates from within our very own flesh. There are a lot of Christians who want to blame all sin in their life on "the enemy," but in truth, most of the everyday sins in our lives originate in our flesh, which is rotten and wicked. Indeed, our flesh can get us into plenty of trouble without the enemy even having to lift a finger.

*For I know that in me (that is, in my flesh) nothing good dwells.* Romans 7:18a *(NKJV)*

Initially we step out into sin because of the desires of our flesh – our desires to feel good and to feel important or powerful. At first, our fleshly desires are satisfied by our sin. But as we continue to practice sin, that is, do it on a regular basis, our sin begins to take over our flesh. This is particularly true of sexual sin. In scripture the Lord points out that sexual sin is different.

*Flee sexual immorality. Every sin that a man does is outside the body, but he who commits sexual immorality sins against his own body.* 1 Corinthians 6:18 *(NKJV)*

There *is* something different about sexual sin and the Lord, in His love for us, warns us of that. Sexual sin is very self-seeking. Other sins, such as alcohol and drug abuse, are as well. These sins are "practiced" because we like the way they make our flesh feel. But herein lies the danger: at some point, our flesh will be overtaken, and we become trapped. We want out, and we know we need to get out, but we are unable to open up the door for the way of escape. How can a person open up a door when her hands are tied? She can't. She must first be untied, in order to turn that doorknob.

I am going to continue on the journey of the downward spiral of sin with you, my friend, because I want you to know fully and truly of the dangers of playing with sin. Your opponent is in this game to win. He is playing for keeps, but the one in sin thinks she is playing for fun. I know that I thought I was playing for fun.

When you travel into spiritual darkness, it damages your soul. My sexual sin is going to cross over into this realm now. What lies ahead describes my trek deeper into the pit of hell and I do not want you to ever actually go there. Please, please do not go there. You do not have to enter into that darkness; it is a choice. Get out before you become trapped. Get out before you become a slave to sin. Without hesitation I share this story with the hope that my life, my testimony, will keep others from stepping further into sin.

# LEAd INTO ObsessiON

In December of 1993 we lived with our girls in Texas, but Scott's job kept him out of town a lot. That year he was working in Ft. Lauderdale, Florida. For Christmas he joined us in Texas, and then I flew back to Ft. Lauderdale with him to stay for a week. My parents kept the girls so I could have an enjoyable week away with my husband. At this point in my marriage, I thought everything was going well. We were watching a lot of pornography together, and had been for quite a while now. To me it seemed that the pornography made our marriage even better. I felt that our physical relationship was great.

On New Year's Eve in Ft. Lauderdale Scott took me to a place he frequented often--a cozy Italian restaurant which had a band and a bar. Despite not being accustomed to drinking alcohol, I allowed myself to become "buzzed" that night. Feeling very in love with my husband, I relaxed and thoroughly enjoyed the delicious food; the dancing, laughing, and drinking; and the attention of the members of the band, who Scott knew very well. I had a marvelous night of fun with my husband that evening. Other patrons even remarked at how in love we seemed. Amazed they asked, "How long have you been married? How many kids do you have? And how is it you both are still so in love?"

But that night when we went back to Scott's apartment he began to ask me questions about one of the band members. He wanted to know if I found this particular man attractive. Well the man *was* very attractive, I was very drunk, and I was already very comfortable in our fantasy games; so it was easy for my husband to now bring this real man into our marriage bed – not physically, but since he was in my mind, in a sense he was there with us. Thus in a figurative sense, my husband and I were now truly involved in sexual immorality.

A few days later we returned to the cozy Italian restaurant and Scott asked this band member to join us at our table. We visited with him at length and when we got home that night Scott again brought him, not physically, but psychologically, into our bedroom. He began to push me further into sin with new sexual ideas in a very different way. We had talked about fantasies many times before but I was sure that those fantasies were never going to come to pass. We would imagine specific scenarios but it was all just a fantasy game that was never going to be

35

played out. I truly believed that neither of us had any desire for what we imagined to actually happen!

At last it was time for me to fly back to Texas and Scott stayed in Ft. Lauderdale working. When I got settled back home, Scott alerted me that he was sending a surprise to me in the mail and that I should be expecting a package soon. Curiously opening the package I was shocked to find inside an 8 X 10 photo of this man from the band along with a cassette tape of his music (he was a singer and played the keyboards). When I explained to Scott that I felt hurt that he, the husband I loved, would send me this, he smoothed things over, persuading me that I should enjoy this man's photo and music as part of my sexual experience. Once again, though I resisted initially, soon I was doing what my husband asked. It was not nearly as difficult to do this time. My husband was out of town and I was lonely. My husband wanted me to do this I rationalized, so what was the big deal? I reasoned that this was just another game that we will play in our marriage; and since I had already watched heaps of pornography, how could this be any different?

With all sincerity I must warn you, if you have not already figured it out, that this sort of fantasy game actually is very, very different from the others. This fantasy involved a real person. I knew this man, had sat in his presence and looked into his eyes. I had spoken with him. Everything about *this game* was different, yet I did not realize that when I first began to play it. My husband encouraged me in this game when we spoke to each other on the phone. Allowing myself to play this game frequently I naively failed to realize I was slipping into real bondage. That little puppy of sin, which had grown into a teenager, was now maturing very quickly. He was a wolf, and he was preparing to come in for the kill; it was just a matter of time now.

When I was in sexual sin, I did not usually attend church. The deeper I was in my sin, the less I went to church. To me it seemed too hypocritical to act spiritual on Sunday, and then to spend the rest of the week avidly enjoying sexual sin. Looking back, I wish that I had kept going to church, because the Word of God is alive and active and it would have made an impact on my spirit. Though I would talk to the Lord about my sin, I was not opening up His Word anymore. By this time I knew I was very deeply in sin, but I liked it. I didn't want to leave it. I was very comfortable in it and it felt good. Naively, I still thought that I could stop whenever I wanted to but I was just not ready to stop yet. I thought that I could just start going back to church whenever I wanted to, and that I could make everything right again when I was ready to stop sinning. Yes, I was very reckless and deceived. There is absolutely nothing that I can say in my defense. Fortunately, my defense comes from the Lord! *So when they continued asking Him, He raised Himself up and said to them, "He who is without sin among you, let him throw a stone at her first."* John 8:7 *(NKJV)*

Upon finishing the typing of this section of my story, I walked into the other room and cried in my husband's arms.

I know I am forgiven completely because the Lord has covered me in His blood. Before the foundations of the earth, He knew the sins that I was going to commit. So why did I cry? I still cannot believe that I did things that I never thought that I was capable of doing. I have asked the Lord to never, ever let me forget what my flesh is capable of doing. My bondage to sexual sin left a scar on my heart and I know it is always going to be there. It is a reminder to me of what my flesh is capable of doing. The scar does not bring me pain because it is completely healed over, but it reminds me always to stay on the narrow path. It reminds me that if I give the enemy an inch, he won't leave me alone until he's taken a mile.

My friends, no one is above sin. In fact, no one is above horrific sins. Do not be deceived: Your flesh is capable of the unspeakable, and if you think otherwise, you are being foolish. As the saying goes, sin always takes you further than you wanted to go; it always keeps you longer than you planned to stay; and it always costs you more than you were willing to pay.

## THE BUTTER VISION

Reader, you and I both need to take a deep breath now and be encouraged in the Lord! I am excited that the Lord directed me to write this book. I love writing it, and I love Him! He always knows exactly what we need, when we need it. He always knows exactly how to minister to His children. Each of us is a unique individual when it comes to our relationship with the Lord. My pastor emphasizes that a lot from the pulpit, citing this verse:

*The LORD looks from heaven; He sees all the sons of men. From the place of His dwelling He looks on all the inhabitants of the earth; He fashions their hearts individually; he considers all their works.* Psalms 33:13-15 *(NKJV)*

You may be married, but you are an individual. You may be a daughter still living at home with your family, but you are an individual. The Lord ministers to us individually because He has fashioned our hearts individually. With that thought in mind, I am going to tell you a God story that the Lord created just for me. He ministered to me in a very individual way, and I know that He wants me to share this with you.

Do you know that God still gives visions to his people in our modern world? Perhaps you believe that visions were only for ancient Bible times. But I know the Lord still gives visions today because He has given me several, and I will be sharing a few of them with you in this book. I did not ask the Lord to give me visions, and I did not expect Him to give me visions. In fact, I really didn't know what they were when the Lord started giving them to me. What I experience seems as if a television show is playing in front of my face, but no screen or set is there.

I don't know why the Lord has chosen to do this in my life, and I realize that this doesn't happen to all of His children. Again, we are individuals and the Lord ministers to each one of us in different ways. A true miracle, my very first vision set me free from my bondage to sexual sin. You will read about it in the pages ahead, as my testimony unfolds. I called it "Divine Deliverance" and to be sure that I would never forget any part of it I wrote down a full description of it a few days after the Lord delivered me in 1995. Since then the Lord has given me other visions of events that subsequently occurred; facts like that cannot be denied or dismissed.

This vision occurred in early April 2011 as I was lying in my current husband's arms one morning before I got out of bed. My husband, Leo, was talking about his illness and his walk with the Lord; as he was speaking, the Lord gave me a very quick vision. I saw a gray serving tray, with a white doily on it, and at the bottom left corner of the tray was a small container of butter. That was it. That is what I saw, and it was as clear as day. It seemed strange to me and I had no idea what the vision could possibly mean. At the time I thought, why in the world would the Lord show me that? I wondered if the picture in my mind was even from the Lord. And I thought these words exactly: "Now that is just weird."

Later I sought the Lord on what I knew He had showed me. Even though it was very odd, I was sure it was from Him because it was presented to me in exactly the same fashion as my other visions. Over the years I have learned to recognize the ways that the Lord speaks to me, and this butter vision certainly felt like Him and looked like Him. I also knew from this verse in Jeremiah 1:13 that the Lord sometimes gives visions that are mundane yet confusing. *And the word of the LORD came to me the second time, saying, "What do you see?" And I said, "I see a boiling pot, and it is facing away from the north." (NKJV)*

My gray serving tray with butter on it did not seem much stranger than Jeremiah's boiling pot facing away from the north. So, I began to attempt to discern what this vision meant. First, I did a Bible study on the word "butter" and found it is mentioned six times in scripture. One of those times was when Abraham served butter to the Lord. Since my butter was on a serving tray, I felt sure that this section of scripture would shed light on the meaning of my vision. I look to scripture to explain everything in my life, and that has served me well.

*And Abraham ran to the herd, took a tender and good calf, gave it to a young man, and he hastened to prepare it. So he took butter and milk and the calf which he had prepared, and set it before them; and he stood by them under the tree as they ate.* Genesis 18:7-8 *(NKJV)*

I just knew that my vision had to have something to do with serving the Lord, but I still did not understand what it really meant. My daughter Krystal knows my relationship with the Lord very well. She understands the ways that the Lord speaks to me, and at times she has even told me things that the Lord has shown me, without my having told her of them. Therefore, I really wanted her insight on this vision. Several times as my daughter Krystal and I jogged together we discussed the vision. Often we laughed heartily while trying to figure it all out. "Maybe the tray means this…. And maybe the butter means this….." Sadly, we remained in the dark regarding the meaning of the butter vision. The Lord had me stumped!

Several weeks had passed since the vision and Krystal was having an outpatient minor medical procedure done at the hospital where I was employed. We had expected to be back home by lunch time, but in the recovery room she was having some unexplained bleeding, so the doctor took her back into the operating room. By the time she had been put to sleep again, they could not find any bleeding and could not even figure out where she had been bleeding. But as a result of this occurrence the doctor wanted Krystal to check into the hospital for observation. She would probably be able to go home that evening the doctor assured us. You will see that by the end of the day I was praising God for that unexplained bleeding! Since we live forty miles from the hospital if they had sent her home at noon, I might have lost my daughter that day.

Several hours passed and Krystal's breathing became very abnormal; the medical staff called it "panting." Noting her respiratory rate was over 60, I went for the nurse and asked her to come to look at Krystal. Within minutes the room was filled with doctors, nurses, a respiratory therapist, and the anesthesiologist who had prepared her for surgery. They told me that she was in anaphylactic shock and that they would have to put her on a respirator because her airways were swelling shut. She was in imminent life-threatening danger; the anesthesiologist said that they didn't even have five minutes to spare and I was ordered to leave the room. But before I left I questioned my daughter, "Krystal there are a lot of people in this room, but who is the most important person in this room with you?" Through very labored breathing she uttered, "Jesus." "You are right, honey," I responded. "Jesus is in this room with you. I have to leave but He is with you. Do not forget that baby."

My husband had left the hospital a few hours earlier and no one in my family was with me. I walked up to the nurses' station knowing that my daughter was being put on a respirator at that very moment. I dropped to my knees, lifted my hands, and began to pray out loud. People were all around me. Since I was an employee of this hospital at that time my coworkers were there also. I addressed myself to all in earshot: "My daughter is in that room but she is not alone. My God is in there with her and my God is right here with me. You can either pray with me or you can ignore me but this is what I do. I am crying out to my God and He is going to take care of her right now." I continued to pray and at that very moment He took over completely; that is, He took over me completely.

I arose to my feet and by this time they had taken Krystal down to the Intensive Care Unit. I was talking to my coworkers and I was totally calm. One of them was very upset and stated she just couldn't understand why I seemed so peaceful and composed. She said that if this was her daughter she would be freaking out. I had the opportunity to tell her all about my Lord as she and I walked to the Intensive Care Unit. Throughout the evening more and more of my coworkers came to check on me and most of them said the same things. As they marveled at the fact I was not utterly distraught, I was able to share with them genuinely about my relationship with the Lord.

Watching a machine breathe for my daughter that day, I knew what Krystal would want me to do during this time. She would want me to rest firmly in the Lord and she would want me to witness to as many people as possible. I also knew what the Lord wanted me to do. He wanted to be glorified in this situation. Since he had taken me over completely at the nurses' station earlier that day, the Holy Spirit was doing all of the talking for me now. I was a vessel in the Hands of Almighty God and I knew it. It was one of the most incredible experiences of my life. I even created a little altar area right there in the hospital room because that is a habit of mine with my Lord. (Don't worry. I have not forgotten that I was telling you about the "butter vision." You will understand soon.)

In the morning they took Krystal off of the respirator but she continued to breathe very rapidly throughout the day. The doctors were starting to express real concern because they felt she should have been improving. It is very difficult to watch your daughter breathe so rapidly for so many hours. Women from my church were in and out of the room and everyone was praying for her. Her breathing became so bad at one point that they prohibited any visitors to her room. But Krystal had been asking for our pastor and he was on his way. He had been there the night before and he was coming to see her again. It seemed like forever to me but at last he arrived. As he spoke to Krystal her breathing began to slow down just a little, but it was still very labored. The pastor stayed with us for a while but finally he had to leave. Right before he left, he and I prayed over her and he anointed her with oil. As we prayed, I felt the power of God in that room in a way that I have never ever felt it before.

Within an hour of our prayer, my daughter was sitting up in a chair taking a few bites of Jello. As the doctor came into the room a nurse was explaining to her that Krystal had been doing badly all day, but rather suddenly in the past hour that had all changed. I delightedly enlightened them about this "all of a sudden" turn for the better! My pastor had come and we had prayed over Krystal and had anointed her with oil. This "treatment" that God prescribes in the Bible (see James 5:14) had quickly brought on this amazing recovery!

That evening Krystal was sleeping soundly at last. If you have ever been in a hospital room for days with a family member who was not doing well, you know what a relief it is when the patient takes a turn for the better; only then you are able, finally, to relax. A friend brought me some grilled chicken from a restaurant and some clean clothes. So I took a hot shower and now was about to eat for the first time since the ordeal began. As I began to eat I looked down at my tray and stared in amazement.

Looking down I saw a gray serving tray, with a white doily on it, and it had butter at the bottom left corner of the tray. Immediately the Lord spoke to my heart, saying, "I went before you, Stacey. I was waiting for you, here in the intensive care unit. I made your path ready. I showed you, and I prepared your way. I will carry you through whatever lies ahead. I am here. My glory is always upon your life, as you serve Me; as you give Me your butter."

I then understood the scripture that the Lord gave me concerning Abraham. Abraham served the Lord his butter. He lived for the Lord and served Him. In the same way, we are to live for the Lord and serve Him. No matter what we are walking through, we are to serve Him at that very moment. Whether it's a moment of joy or a moment of pain, He has already gone before us and has prepared our way. He will never leave us or forsake us. We are always to bow before Him and serve Him with our lives. His glory will fall upon us, and He will give us the strength to face whatever is put in front of us.

The Lord spoke to me again that Monday night after we came home from the hospital. I was weeping in His arms and He said, "Stacey, when you bowed down at the nurses' station as they were putting Krystal on the respirator, praying out loud in front of everyone, with arms lifted to Me, that was you serving Me your butter. Tell everyone at Wild Ride to serve Me their butter."

I knew His message was that we must give Him our best. We must give Him our butter. When we do this, He gets all the glory.

Wild Ride Ministries is the name of the church where I worship in Harper, Texas. Yes, that is an unusual name. Before I began attending the church, I used to drive by the sign at the church office thinking, "Wild Ride? What kind of a church could that possibly be?" Providentially, a friend asked me to come to Wild Ride when she was to be baptized there one Sunday in November 2008. I attended the church service that day and have worshiped there regularly ever since.

My pastor teaches directly from the Word of God and the Holy Spirit has definitely anointed him. When you set foot on our church property you feel the presence of Almighty God! The people who attend Wild Ride love one another with the love of the Lord. As a bull rider involved in ministry to the cowboy community for many years, my pastor preached and shared the Word of God at rodeos using "Wild Ride" as the name of his ministry organization. When the ministry in Harper developed into a church, the parishioners wanted to keep the name of the pastor's rodeo ministry. Thus, Wild Ride Ministries is the name of my church and I absolutely love everything about it. We actually have a rodeo arena on our property! I know, only in Texas!

## Trust Betrayed

My husband's job in Ft. Lauderdale was extended and he and I decided that our family should relocate to Florida. We decided to wait until the school year ended so in June of 1994 the girls and I moved to South Florida. Since I was only accustomed to small-town life, living in South Florida was quite a cultural shock for me. Scott was making very good money so he and I enjoyed going out almost every weekend to restaurants and clubs, dancing, dining and drinking. The scenery was beautiful, the city was filled with activity, and I was crazy in love with my husband. I remember thinking at that time that this was one of the greatest times of my life. As messed up as it sounds, I thought that my husband and I had a very special relationship. I knew our physical relationship was probably different from what other married couples experienced, but Scott always assured me that it was okay as long as we, as a couple, agreed about it. We were still watching pornography on a regular basis and that guy from the band was still a part of our life, because we visited that restaurant often.

One Friday night Scott told me that we were going to South Beach in Miami to go out to eat with one of his friends. I assumed his friend, Mark, would have a girlfriend with him but he was alone when we met him at his house. The three of us went out to eat and had a lively, fun time together. Mark told us all about his job. He was a fascinating guy with a dynamic personality. Though Scott had been friends with him for a while, this was the first time that I had ever met him. While we ate at the restaurant everything seemed normal, and never during that time did I have any sexual thoughts towards Mark.

When we arrived back at Mark's home, as soon as Mark and I walked through his front door, Scott shut the door behind me. My husband was standing outside and I was inside the house with Mark, who came toward me to kiss me. "Stop!" I yelled, but he insisted that this is what my husband wanted. Then Scott started speaking to me through the door, acknowledging that he had planned for this to happen.

I'm sure you've heard of the expression "being eaten alive." That is exactly how I felt at that moment. Whatever was left of the Stacey who grew up in a small town in Texas died right then and there in Mark's foyer. I must have been in shock; I remember feeling numb, as if death had come over me. Yet I was still alive and breathing. I was astonished at what my husband had just done to me and I went through the motions with Mark as if a robot. Desperately I begged Scott to open up the door and to come inside, which, finally, he did. Scott joined in on the sexual activity. I still marvel that though I did not enjoy this kind of sexual sin in which I was participating, I didn't do anything to stop it.

We drove home after this event in complete silence. Scott attempted to talk to me but I sat as mute as a stone. I will never forget rolling down my window and looking up at the sky, driving down I-95. I whispered, "Jesus, what has happened to me?" The tears began to stream down my face. At that moment, I realized how very lost I was, how very messed up I had become. And at that moment, I also knew I had to do something to get out of this sinful sexual lifestyle. For the first time in my marriage I thought about leaving my husband. Unfortunately, I did not have enough courage or strength to get out right away, and the downward spiral continued.

Perhaps as you read this part of my story you are thinking, "Why did you not stop this Stacey?" Yesterday as I drove into my driveway that is exactly what I was thinking, as I anticipated writing down this part of my story. I began to cry, asking, "Why Lord? Why did I let these things happen to me?" Quickly came His answer: "Your mind was not healthy." I felt Him hold me in His arms comforting me as I sat in my driveway. It was so true--my mind was not healthy at all. The months and years of using fantasies, self-sex, sexual devices and pornography had been destroying my mind and in fact, the very fabric of my being.

The experience of writing down my story--the events and the feelings that constituted my life of sexual sin--has been sincerely enlightening. Though I had put all these things in my past and have been walking in complete forgiveness for many years, as I have been writing down the story (the *details*), the Lord has been speaking to me. He has been revealing truths concerning sexual sin to me. I sense He is writing this book for me. I sit at the computer, and I allow Him to move me by His Spirit. But back to the story...

Scott and I had been watching pornography for months, and most pornographic films involve more than just two people. I suppose I really should not have been amazed that my husband wanted to "play out" what we had been watching. Simply put, he wanted the fantasy to become reality and he manipulated events to make that happen. His mind was very unhealthy; he was even more lost than I was. Who, if in his right mind, would want to watch another man kiss his wife? No man in his right mind wants that. It was exactly as the Lord reminded me, "Your mind was not healthy."

*For those who live according to the flesh set their minds on the things of the flesh, but those who live according to the Spirit, the things of the Spirit. For to be carnally minded is death, but to be spiritually minded is life and peace.* Romans 8:5-6 *(NKJ)*

As I now know only too well, what you think about affects you. In fact, our thoughts can even determine who we become. Since my husband and I filled our thoughts, through our eyes and ears, with perversion, we became perverted. You may be toying with impure thoughts inside of your mind, thinking that it's no big deal and that you are still in control of your mind. But having been there myself I am here to testify to you that if you do not submit your thought-life to godly control (in the sense of "taking every thought captive to the obedience of Christ" II Cor 10:5) then your thoughts will eventually control your mind, and then your entire being. You will end up doing things that you never ever thought that you would be capable of doing. Indeed, the battle is won or lost in the mind. Because my mind was on a steady diet of unholy, twisted material, I was losing the battle and things became much worse, very quickly.

Now that I was emotionally numb, darkness took me over even more. It would be several months before I talked to the Lord again. Though I knew He was with me through this period, I refused to look at Him or even glance towards Him. Knowing I was filthy in my sin, I could not bring myself to look at Him. But He never took His eyes off of me. He knew exactly what I was going to do before He even breathed life into me.

*Your eyes saw my substance, being yet unformed. And in Your book they all were written, the days fashioned for me, when as yet there were none of them.* Psalms 139:16 *(NKJV)*

I should have looked at Him and reached for Him. He was there to comfort, rescue and forgive me. Actually, He had already forgiven me. He did that for me on the Cross. Fortunately, I knew enough to know that He was my way of escape. But knowing what I needed to do was not the same as doing it, and I persisted in my sinful lifestyle a while longer.

I had been angry with my husband in the past about his pressuring me into doing certain sexual sins, but something changed that night. The word angry no longer could describe what I was feeling. I was becoming enraged. You are probably thinking, "Finally!" But what I have learned is that if you do not handle your anger correctly, in Christ, the enemy will have a field day with the anger that is in your heart.

*"Be angry, and do not sin": do not let the sun go down on your wrath, nor give place to the devil.* Ephesians 4:26-27 *(NKJV)*

I had every right to be outraged at my husband for taking me to this man's house and for this path that he shoved me down. From that night forward, being both numb and angry, I did give place to the devil. My husband continued to pressure me into another kind of sexual sin, as you will read, but this time I ran toward the sin full speed ahead, because I was furious. My attitude became, "You want me to do this? Fine! Does that make you happy now?!" If I could, I wanted to make him feel the hurt that I felt because of the way he treated me.

As this story unfolds even further, you will see how my anger towards my husband took on a life of its own. To me, the worst sins I did were the ones I did voluntarily and when he was not present. I guess you could say he trained me well.

To give you a fuller picture of the way we were polluting our minds, there are a few other things I will tell you. When I moved to Florida to be with my husband, he and I also started going to strip clubs. Since I had been watching women in the pornographic videos, what I saw in the strip clubs was nothing new to me. And believe it or not, there were a lot of other women in those clubs, like me, being entertained alongside their husbands or boyfriends. Scott had also been urging me for months to mess around with women; such behavior was featured in all the pornography that we had been watching.

Another thing that was taking place was that my collection of sexual devices was multiplying; I had a whole box full of them. And, there was a married man who lived directly behind our house who began to take notice of me as I was sunbathing in my backyard. I was there every day at the same time. He began to show up when I was there and he eventually started talking to me on occasion. Our kitchen windows were directly across from each other and often I could see him watch me in the evenings when I was washing the dishes. Not surprisingly, Scott got a kick out of this. In addition, I had started taking classes to become a personal trainer. I befriended a cop in the class, who I had noticed could not take his eyes off me, and as we teamed up together on some course assignments he began to open up to me about his life. At the time, he was separated from his wife for the third time. Putting myself in these various compromising situations, I nearly guaranteed that I would be led further into sin. That's the way it works: Sin rises up in your life like yeast; under favorable conditions, just a pinch can grow into a very large batch of dough.

*You ran well. Who hindered you from obeying the truth? This persuasion does not come from Him who calls you. A little leaven leavens the whole lump.* Galatians 5:7-9 *(NKJV)*

## Pit Stop

Before I continue further with my downward spiral, and my God stories, I would like to take a few minutes to tell you what is going on inside of my heart, in my life right now. I never knew that the Lord was going to call me to write this book, and since He did call, I must be obedient. Recounting and describing the baser, more immoral things I did is affecting me in the present. I have cried more than I thought I would. I so much want to get to the deliverance part of my story, but, as I've told you, the Lord specifically directed me to share the details of my sin.

I was just sitting outside on my back porch swing looking up at the stars and having a conversation with my God. He is the God of Abraham, Isaac, and Jacob, and He is also the God of Stacey. I love calling Him the God of Abraham, Isaac, and Jacob. It has become a little joke between me and my daughter. When Krystal sees me here and comes to ask me what I am doing as I lie on the trampoline, looking up at the sky, she knows that I will say I am talking to the "God of Abraham, Isaac, and Jacob." Anyway, I was telling my God that He is going to have to give me the strength to complete this writing task, because it is becoming a lot harder than I ever expected.

I was trying to explain to my second husband what is going on inside of me as I write my story, but I found it remarkably hard for me to put into words. I told him that this experience is not a bad thing, but it's a very deep thing, and I didn't know how to describe it to him. I have not told you much about my second husband yet, but you will get to know him much better as my testimony unfolds. I will tell you this: he is a very faith-filled, godly man. He had to be in order to be able to trust me, knowing of my past. Only a truly devout Christian can really comprehend the complete forgiveness of sin that only Jesus provides. My second husband, Leo, only knows me as Stacey who is "Crazy for Christ." I was wearing that phrase on my baseball cap the day that he first spoke to me at the park. By God's grace, Leo completely sees me through the eyes of Christ.

As I was trying to explain to Leo what I had been experiencing as I wrote, he said, "The Lord is doing a final healing and purging concerning your sexual sin." I looked up purge in the dictionary and found that it means "to clean" and "to empty." In his abundant grace and mercy, God gave me a husband of great wisdom and discernment, who knows me well and recognizes how the Lord works with me! Healing and purging is exactly what is taking place, I just did not know what to call it. The Lord is completely emptying me of this baggage by having me write it all down in a very detailed manner. The Lord is doing a thorough cleansing in my soul in a much deeper way than He ever has, concerning my sexual sin.

I have always been thankful I was able to receive forgiveness and move on past all of this sin years ago, especially for the sake of my precious daughters who needed God-honoring parents to lead and teach them. But now that they are grown up, the Lord is going to redeem what Satan meant for evil in my life; He is going to turn it around and use it for His work and His glory. I am now confident of His plan and purpose in all of this. He wants women to know that there is hope for them; that there is cleansing and healing for them; and that they are not alone in their sexual sin. Many modern women are engaged in or dabbling with this type of sin, and I am happy to be here to tell you that the victory is yours in Christ Jesus.

## Prayer of Faith

Now let me encourage you with a God story concerning prayer and faith. Leo and I had been married for a little over six months when he became ill and his sickness affected all aspects of our life. One thing the Lord has showed me over the years is that whenever drastic things begin to happen in your physical world, then you better do some radical things in your spiritual world. I decided to commit to pray for an hour every morning for a month. At first I thought, "How is this even possible? What and how can I pray for a whole hour?" But I set my alarm for an hour earlier and I just began to do it. Within a week, I found that I was able to pray for an hour very easily. In fact, it was incredible spending that much concentrated time every morning with the Lord. One of the things that I was praying for was for the Lord to provide a new place for my family to live. My husband had lost his job because of his sickness and we no longer could afford the home we were living in. I asked the Lord to please provide a place for us to live for $500 a month and I asked for a house, not an apartment. I knew that when we pray, we should pray very specifically. But remember, we lived in South Florida, so essentially I was praying for the impossible. Everything advertised in the paper was at least $1,200 a month. But I just knew that my God was going to do it somehow, some way.

*'Ah, Lord GOD! Behold, You have made the heavens and the earth by Your great power and outstretched arm. There is nothing too hard for You.* Jeremiah 32:17 *(NKJV)*

The world would say "Never" but I trusted that my God would say, "I am going to bless you, My daughter, because you make Me smile." That is the way I believe my Father thinks of me. Anyone who knows me well knows I never do anything halfheartedly. Nope; I go all out. I went all out in my sin, and now I go all out for my God! Do you believe that we can actually please our Lord? Do you know that we can actually put a smile on His face?

*But without faith it is impossible to please Him, for he who comes to God must believe that He is, and that He is a rewarder of those who diligently seek Him.* Hebrews 11:6 *(NKJV)*

Most certainly, I had the faith. I did not know how He was going to do it but I just knew that He would do it. As I continued to seek him diligently, one day He showed up. As the world would tell it, my husband "just happened" to be at the right place at the right time; but in reality, the Lord placed my husband in a hallway, in one of our church's seven buildings, so that he overheard some men talking about who they might find to rent a missionary's home. The missionary was only asking that his monthly mortgage payment be paid to the bank. Leo spoke up and that day we signed a contract to rent that house in South Florida for $527 a month! (I cut the Lord some slack for that extra $27!) God is willing to do the impossible, but the question is, are you willing to believe for the impossible? Are you willing to step out in complete, reckless abandoned faith and ask Him for the impossible? There is nothing too hard for our God, as long as it lines up with His Will.

I do want to caution, however, that we should choose carefully what we pray for. I believe that as we seek the Lord in prayer, the Holy Spirit actually impresses things upon our heart to pray for. He leads us in the right direction, we begin to pray for things in line with His Will, and then He answers our prayers. And if it is God's will, He will do it. He always knows the end from the beginning. He was the one who gave me the thought to pray for a house in South Florida for $500 a month. I love how God works by His Spirit!

*'Call to Me, and I will answer you, and show you great and mighty things, which you do not know.'* Jeremiah 33:3 *(NKJV)*

I was actually reading that verse this morning and something caught my eye that I have never noticed before. In this verse the word "mighty" also means "inaccessible." So, He will show us things we don't have access to otherwise. That is, it's only by Him and through Him that we are shown these things; *He* is our access. He is the only way that certain things can happen in our lives, and He tells us to call on Him for these things. By His Spirit, He leads us to the inaccessible. He has access to all things because He is the One who orchestrates all things! I don't know about you, but that gets me tremendously excited. We serve a very thrilling God and we should have enthusiasm overflowing from within us. Christians should be bursting with joy, even when life is hard. We should wake up every day overflowing with the joy of the Lord.

*Do not sorrow, for the joy of the LORD is your strength.* Nehemiah 8:10b *(NKJV)*

Fall more in love with Jesus TODAY!

# FOUR
## Bondage Continues

### Vile Passions

Concerning this book my pastor advised me, "Be sure to just write what the Lord speaks, and all will be well." I typed up that sentence and posted it on the wall next to my computer so that I am constantly reminded of this counsel as I work. This next story is very dark but I know that there are women living in this darkness. As tempting as it is to leave out this section, I know that the Lord wants me to share it with you. I believe very few Christian women would be willing to share such a story about themselves in any setting. But I am very zealous for the Lord, and I am very forgiven, so I will share it with the hope that any who have committed this type of sin will be set free and healed.

In the weeks after our visit to Mark's house my husband, having noted how that event had affected me, was showing extraordinary thoughtfulness and kindness toward me. For a while, he and I spent more time at our home with our four little girls, playing with them in our swimming pool, having backyard picnics and just enjoying life as a family. From the outside looking in, we appeared to be a normal family. My girls loved their daddy and he loved them. People took notice of our family everywhere we went: there were so many girls, and we all have very light blonde hair. The oldest girls are identical twins and the younger two girls looked so much alike at that time people often asked if they were twins as well. We were a family, and as messed up as my marriage was becoming, this was *my* family, so it was very precious to me.

As I considered leaving my husband of nine years, I agonized that I would be splitting up this precious family also. Scott definitely did not want to leave me. I pondered, "How could I leave him? How could I do that to my girls?" Also, I knew that I had never worked outside my home since I gotten married. It was my desire to be at home to raise our girls and to provide a welcoming, comfortable home for my husband. Working outside my home had never interested me. I was acutely apprehensive about leaving Scott, realizing that if I did, every aspect of my life would change. I questioned if I was ready to make such drastic changes, if I was capable and strong enough to succeed, and if I was really willing to take away from my girls their daddy. Should I just put up with this bizarre sexual stuff, I deliberated?

Scott and I went out on the town again. This time we went to a club with another of his friends, but this friend did have a girlfriend. As we all danced and drank, Scott persistently urged me to kiss this girl. As the evening wore on, Scott kept pressuring me about this, and as a result, I was becoming increasingly, intensely annoyed. The friend's girlfriend and I went into the restroom together and I told her that my husband was insisting that I kiss her, and that I just didn't understand why this was so important to him. Her response shocked me: She said that we should do it for him. It was no big deal to her, she claimed; in fact, she thought her boyfriend would probably get a kick out of it too.

As I mentioned earlier, a part of me had become completely numb and my attitude towards my husband had become, "Fine! Does this make you happy now?" So in my numbness, and out of my anger (somehow these two can coincide together) I kissed this girl in front of my husband and her boyfriend. We were all drunk, and before the night ended, it was more than just a kiss that I shared with this woman.

Am I what the world calls bi-sexual? Am I a lesbian? No, but I am a sinner who was entangled in sexual sin and I took a nose dive that night. My mind was not healthy; it had become debased. But there was something different about this sin; something much different about it and I knew it immediately. I was very reluctant to kiss the girl, and I only did it out of frustration and rage. But as soon as I stepped into this sin, as I kissed that girl, my flesh instantly entered into a different type of demonic world. It is hard to describe, but Paul's words in the verses below do come close to expressing what I felt in that event.

53

*Therefore God also gave them up to uncleanness, in the lusts of their hearts, to dishonor their bodies among themselves, who exchanged the truth of God for the lie, and worshiped and served the creature rather than the Creator, who is blessed forever. Amen. For this reason God gave them up to vile passions. For even their women exchanged the natural use for what is against nature. Likewise also the men, leaving the natural use of the woman, burned in their lust for one another, men with men committing what is shameful, and receiving in themselves the penalty of their error which was due. And even as they did not like to retain God in their knowledge, God gave them over to a debased mind, to do those things which are not fitting.* Romans 1:24-28 (NKJV)

In particular, the phrase, "God gave them up to vile passions," seems to convey what I felt happened that night. It does not mean that God gave up on me. The experience of having sexual activity with two men was obviously a very immoral thing to do, but intimate sexual contact with another woman was at a whole new level of depravity. It is something that you just don't do—a line that you just do not cross. It was something that "I would never do in a million years," but I did do it. And perhaps because it was SO taboo, this new-for-me sin was exceptionally enticing to my flesh. Now that I have admitted to this act, perhaps you doubt if I truly was a Christian at that time. I assure you, I was. Certainly I was carnal and backsliding in a monumental way, but I knew Jesus and He knew me. He knew my name; it was written in His book. I was His daughter, but sadly, I was a very, very disturbed daughter.

Though I only practiced the sin of homosexual activity a few times, I now understand the trap the enemy lays for humans concerning this sin, because I have experienced it. I understand how the enemy plays with our minds through the lies promoted in the popular culture. He leads people trapped in this kind of sin to believe that they are "gay" or "bi-sexual," that this is the way they were born, that this is "OK" and that they have no control over their desires. Our crafty enemy uses tricks from hell to make them believe they are attracted to the same sex due to their body chemistry, and that "It's not your fault." He lies to them, insisting, "You would not be attracted to persons of the same sex unless you were born that way." I beg you, if you are trapped in this sin, please *stop listening to the lies.* I understand the power that this sin has because I lived in it, but our God is far more powerful. He has created a way out for you, and that way out is Jesus Christ, His Son.

This type of sin is very commanding; it took control of my thought life very quickly and it took many months for my mind to recover to the point that this sin no longer tempted me. I can remember being in the women's locker room at a gym and having to recite scriptures to myself in order to resist the "temptations" around me. I felt disgusted by this, reminding myself, "This is truly ridiculous Stacey; being tempted by such a thing as this." I am thankful to report for a long time now this sin is something that never tempts me at all. Naturally I face temptations just like everyone else, but I no longer have to quote scriptures for being tempted in this area!

Since this was a part of my journey in my downward spiral of sin, I chose to relate this wretched experience to you so God can redeem it. I pray He can use what I learned through all this to minister to other women who are struggling in this area and to bring glory to Himself.

*"But as for you, you meant evil against me; but God meant it for good, in order to bring it about as it is this day, to save many people alive.* Genesis 50:20 *(NKJV)*

## The Foundation Crumbles

Several weeks later my husband and I went out to dinner and then to a club. Scott ordered a few drinks but uncharacteristically he did not want to dance. In fact he was very somber, and I could tell something was wrong. I will never forget that night. As we stood leaning against the wall beside the dance floor, Scott leaned in to speak to me. The music was so loud I assumed that I must have misheard him, so I yelled, "What did you say?" The foundation of my life collapsed when he repeated, "I slept with another woman." At that moment the world I had known and believed was real for over 15 years came to an abrupt end.

Utterly astonished, I stood silently and listened to him describe how it happened, when it happened, and why it happened. I remember feeling as if time itself had stopped and I was watching everything in my life come crashing down around me. Crying and very apologetic, he explained that the woman had been mailing letters to our home but that so far he had intercepted them before I had checked the mail. He admitted that he had been with her several times; he knew that he had to tell me about the affair before she did. Still in shock, and under the influence of alcohol, I told him that I forgave him, and promised that we would work through this.

But I didn't feel the same way when I awoke the next morning with the alcohol now out of my blood stream. Lying in bed silently, I opened my eyes and started recalling all the things that I had done for him—for his pleasure. I remembered arguing about and opposing the immoral activities he was so insistent upon, and yet finally giving in to what he wanted. I couldn't stop thinking of the words he had used countless times to reassure me: *This is just between us.* To top it off, the adultery had taken place in our bed, the one I was lying on at that very moment. Tears began to pour out from within me. The pure and total trust that I had in my husband had been shattered, thus destroying the foundation of my marriage. I felt that day that I must have been the foremost fool in all the world.

You see, everything that I had done--all of the sexual sins that I was so reticent to commit--I did to please him. I can't say that he forced me; he never held a gun to my head; he never hit me or threatened to hurt me, or to leave me, if I didn't do any of those sexual things. But he coaxed and cajoled, relentlessly, until he got his way. I have to admit that I freely made the choices to enter those sins, but I did it because I loved him and I trusted him with my whole life. I had loved him since I was thirteen years old. He was the one who held my whole world in his hands. He was the one who had my whole heart. He was the father of my four little girls. And he had maintained that as long as he and I both agreed, what we were doing was acceptable for a Christian couple. He believed that it was *our* physical relationship, as husband and wife, and we could fashion it as we pleased.

If you read the paragraph above carefully, you will see the source of my downfall. Quite simply, I put my man above my God in every facet of my life. I knew, every step of the way, even as early as when we started using fantasies together, that my husband was leading me into sin. I justified our sexual sins in my mind, because, after all, this was my *husband*, and I can trust him with my life.

I know, my dear friend, that you must be thinking, "Of course he slept with another woman Stacey. Look at the things he was having you do!" But I must be completely honest with you—since that is what this entire story is all about. I really believed that he would be faithful to me sexually. I thought I could trust him *because* we had such an unconventional sexual relationship. Since we were doing all the wild things he thought and imagined, why would he not be satisfied with me and me alone? I was doing everything he wanted, even things that I did not want to do.

I guess you could say I was a sucker who fell right into the enemy's hands because I was so trusting with my husband in the marriage bed. Not wise in the ways of the world, and naïve about the ways of sin, I was easily deceived into thinking that Scott would never betray me because I had given him virtually unrestricted control over my physical body. My marriage bed was full of sexual sin and sin never satisfies. I now recognize that *of course* my husband had sex with another woman because that is the way that sin works—sin grows, destroys, and devours. The enemy used an arsenal of corrupt weapons to destroy my marriage: fantasies, sexual devices, self-sex, pornography, group sex, and bi-sexual activities. These are all demonic tools the enemy uses to destroy relationships.

Before my story is done I will teach you the godly tools you need to fight against sexual sin. Those essential skills are included in the deliverance part of my testimony, and I cannot wait to get there! But first I will relate a few more stories that occurred along the downward spiral of sexual sin before I hit rock bottom, from which point I finally looked up. (Some of us just refuse to stop until we beat ourselves up so badly that we can barely breathe.) I have to confess that the next sins I will recount to you are ones that I committed all on my own. Though I was both devastated by and enraged at my husband, instead of running to my Lord, I ran away from Him, to the world, seeking at least some sort of satisfaction through revenge. I ran straight to what I knew, and what I knew was the sexual world.

But first, something pleasant...

## Worship through Running

This God story is a little different from those that I have already communicated to you. Rather than a particular event or day of my life, it's about a part of my daily life; after all, in my opinion, each and every day is a God story. A God story doesn't have to involve car keys miraculously disappearing then reappearing out of nowhere, a van falling from heaven, or even the sudden collapse of a bed! The greatest God story of all is the daily personal relationship that each of us can have with the Lord.

I have mentioned to you that I am a runner. At this point I want to explain how the Lord has used running in my life. Have you ever felt like you could have a *spiritual* nervous breakdown? Not a *mental* breakdown, but a *spiritual* breakdown. Let me attempt to explain what I mean by asking another question. Has the Lord ever pushed you beyond what you thought you were spiritually capable of handling? Has He ever orchestrated circumstances in your life that seemed impossible for you to manage or survive? This may sound crazy, but for a period of about 2 years, that is how I felt. The dynamics of my life were so overwhelming I sometimes felt I must be living in a Bible story! Finally, I knew that I could not continue to live in that place of turmoil. I had to make a decision.

Whenever crushing events occur in your life, a decision must be made. Are you going to rise up to walk on the path that the Lord has set before you, or are you going to give up, turn around and go in the other direction because the Lord's path is too tough? A remarkable revelation that the Lord has given me is this: the details in our lives are a result of the decisions that we make. In sharing the specifics of the downward spiral of sexual sin that occurred in my life I have pointed out to you that I made some very ungodly decisions along the way. Praise the Lord my story does not end there! When I started making God-led decisions, the details of my life changed drastically.

During this period of my potential spiritual breakdown I came to realize that I had to rise up to what God wanted from me and stop whining like a baby. Fortunately I had enough wisdom to know that things in our lives will not get better unless we first make changes. So I changed the essential things concerning my walk with the Lord: I began to pray more, worship more, read the Word more, fast on a regular basis, and I began to run. I had been a certified National Strength & Conditioning Association Personal Trainer for over ten years and so I fully understood that our spiritual, mental and physical facets interact with one another, and all three aspects must be in good health for optimal functioning.

The Lord created our human bodies with those three parts, and yet we are one body, a reflection of the Trinity. In my as-yet unpublished book <u>Heavenly Fitness</u> I expound on these three aspects of our lives. (The Lord told me to put that book aside for now, to pursue writing and publishing this book.)

I had not run in years but I began to run, beginning with very short distances. I was a frightful sight to see, often gasping for breath after running less than fifty yards! But I dedicated my running time to the Lord, making sure that I got out of the house and spent time with Him in prayer, while exercising. I forced myself to do it because I knew that it would make me stronger spiritually, and I realized what I needed was spiritual growth. Also, I knew that the running would help me feel better physically and mentally. My short runs gradually increased in length and after two months I was running at least two miles several times a week; and, more important, my spirit was growing by leaps and bounds.

For me running became a form of worship. Through running I was breaking the strength of my flesh. Yes, even though I was actually building up my physical strength, in another sense I was breaking down my "spiritual flesh," the flesh that can become tempted. I liken running to fasting. In fasting, you are denying your body the food it wants. You feel hungry but tell your flesh "no." Your flesh weakens, while your spirit strengthens. In my running, I am denying my flesh comfort. My tired body asks me to please stop, but my spirit refuses to comply. It may seem unusual, but running has been a key factor in my spiritual growth. Running has played a crucial role in my dying to my flesh; it has made me able to stand strong spiritually, resisting temptations to sin in deed, word or thought.

Before I began typing this book, I usually ran two to four miles, at least three times a week. Though I certainly didn't plan it this way, since I began working on this book, I have been running longer distances. Writing this book has been a great challenge on several levels, and I have really needed the additional spiritual strength that has grown in me through the increased running. Often lately I go out and run four to eight miles, praising the Lord every step of the way. Incredibly, one day I accomplished a goal I had had for quite some time by running from my home to my church, an 11-mile journey.

My dear friend, I pray that regardless of what is taking place in your life right now, you will discover ways to grow in your spirit and die to your flesh. I pray you will know that each and every day is a God story and you will fully apprehend that the Lord longs to spend time with you. Be creative in your relationship with Him and make your relationship with Him an amazing God story every day! Delight yourself in Him every day, and you will grow spiritually stronger than you ever could have imagined.

I have a little prayer box in which I place mementos that carry special significance in my relationship with the Lord. They are the things that I place on my altar before the Lord. I like to create a very personal worship environment for Him and myself. It is very intimate, unique and private. I know He doesn't require this of me, but I go to extremes for my Lord because He goes to extremes for me! He died for me. He rose from the dead for me. He forgives me of all my sins. He truly and perfectly loves me. In my opinion, it does not get any more extreme than that!

*Delight yourself also in the LORD, and He shall give you the desires of your heart. Commit your way to the LORD, trust also in Him, and He shall bring it to pass.* Psalms 37:4-5 *(NKJV)*

## Seventh Commandment

Though I had committed all sorts of sexually immoral acts with my husband in the nine years we had been married, his confession of adultery just exploded my world and in trying to devise some way to get back at him, I ran straight to what I knew, and what I knew was the sexual arena.

I still had Mark's business card in my purse, the card that my husband had given me that night we were at Mark's house in Miami. Mark had called me a few days after that event took place, wanting assurance that I was okay, since he had observed that the activities of that night had upset me greatly. He explained that he had thought Scott had informed me of the agenda for that evening, but as things progressed he could see that it was a surprise to me.

Within a few weeks of learning of my husband's affair, I had arranged to meet with Mark in South Beach, Miami. I told him about Scott's affair and that it was my desire to "finish what we started that night at his home" but that I did not want my husband to be a part of it. I was feeling very hurt, and very angry; since I was already comfortable with Mark, he seemed to me to be the perfect person with whom to have my "revenge sex." I lied to my husband about where I was going and, completely of my own volition, that night I committed adultery.

It may surprise you to know that I didn't experience any feelings of guilt or shame. I knew that I was a very wretched sinner and that I was completely turning my back on God. *This* sin I had committed without any urging from Scott (or Mark); no, this was all my idea. I was now an adulteress. Even though I was aware of having a way out before I did this sinful act, rebelliously I chose not to take it. The truth is, I was angry with God. I realized that because He is all-knowing, God knew on the day I said my wedding vows that my husband was going to lead me into sexual idolatry, and that he was going to commit adultery. I was placing blame on God, instead of on the human sinners in this story. Actually, I felt betrayed by my husband and betrayed by God. Looking back, I see how tragic it is that I believed such a lie. My mind was deluded because of the overwhelming presence of sin. God was there to protect me the whole time; it was I who betrayed Him.

Even when I wasn't plotting revenge, I was a very troubled twenty-seven-year-old with four little girls to care for. I mention my girls because I always went home to them. I committed these horrible sinful acts, and then I went home to look into the eyes of my precious daughters. It seemed everything around me, and everything inside of me was dying, but I couldn't die no matter how badly I wanted to. I had to keep going every day, no matter what I was feeling, because these little girls needed the love of their mom, and their mom just needed to be loved. At this time of my life, I didn't have a true understanding of what real love was, and in particular I had no comprehension of healthy, God-ordained love between a husband and wife. I thought I knew, but what I believed was all a lie.

To this day, it is still hard for me to believe that I committed adultery. It's just not me. But I did do those things, I did travel down that very dark path. Miraculously, I cannot remember having sexual intercourse with Mark, but I know that I did. The Lord has graciously removed that memory from my mind completely. I only realized that recently, because

I had not thought of any of these things until I started writing this book. I had never tried to remember, because I had no reason to remember. Since the Lord is having me now share the details of my story, I did try to remember, but in his everlasting mercy The Lord has so completely delivered me that I cannot even remember what happened. The Lord scattered my sin, as far as the East is from the West, and then my mind forgot my sin; a perfect combination!

*For as the heavens are high above the earth, so great is His mercy toward those who fear Him; As far as the east is from the west, so far has He removed our transgressions from us.* Psalms 103:11-12 *(NKJV)*

*Brethren, I do not count myself to have apprehended; but one thing I do, forgetting those things which are behind and reaching forward to those things which are ahead, I press toward the goal for the prize of the upward call of God in Christ Jesus.* Philippians 3:13-14 *(NKJV)*

During this time Scott was still living with me, but we were having a lot of problems because of all the sexual sin. Of course I already knew about his affair, and I confessed to him the day after I committed adultery. I begged him that we stop the pornography and all the fantasies. The only way that our marriage will ever be healed, I implored him, is if we were to stop this immoral sex.

We did make attempts to stop these activities, but our physical relationship was still very warped because it was not Christ-centered. (I know that may sound strange, but it is nevertheless true that your sexual relationship with your husband should always be Christ-centered.) One night, while I was having ungodly sex with my husband (with the box of sexual devices next to the bed), I heard a spiritual voice speak to me. But it was not the still, small voice of the Lord. Loudly, in my mind, I heard the voice command me, "Do what I say, and I will give you whatever you want." The sex that I was having was not intimate sex, and after it was over, I began to sob intensely. I cried to my husband that sex had destroyed our marriage and that we didn't have any idea about what real love was. We had walked away from the Lord and now everything was destroyed. I accused him of taking me away from Jesus and I threw the box of sexual devices across the room. "I hate this," I screamed. "I hate this! These toys, all of this stuff, has destroyed me."

That was the first time I had ever heard a spiritual voice and those words, are etched in my mind, "Do what I say, and I will give you whatever you want." Don't they sound familiar? Look at this verse:

*Again, the devil took Him up on an exceedingly high mountain, and showed Him all the kingdoms of the world and their glory. And he said to Him, "All these things I will give You if You will fall down and worship me." Then Jesus said to him, "Away with you, Satan! For it is written, 'You shall worship the Lord your God, and Him only you shall serve.'" Then the devil left Him, and behold, angels came and ministered to Him.* Matthew 4:8-11 *(NKJV)*

By no means am I comparing myself to Jesus, or saying that Satan himself addressed me. But and I am certain a demon spoke to me. I believe he was enticing me to walk down *his* path and promising he would give me whatever I wanted. At that time, what I had been yearning for was a sexual encounter with the man from the band who Scott had introduced me to on New Year's Eve. So I realized immediately what this demonic message meant.

The voice sounded very evil and harsh, and yet was also enticing. Since I was a Christian, I recognized that being able to hear a demonic voice meant I was coming very close to the edge of hell. This voice awakened me somewhat to how deeply entrenched in sin I was. I understood that Satan was really out to get me, but why? I was just a small-town girl from Texas. My life was already totally screwed up, so why was he going out of his way to speak to me? I thought about this for days. "Do what I say, and I will give you whatever you want." I began to talk to Jesus again. I didn't want to hear that other voice ever again.

Though I began to talk to Jesus, I still had not bowed down to Him, nor surrendered my life, my heart and my flesh, back to Him. My flesh was thriving, since I had been feeding it excessively for years. At that time, I didn't understand the spiritual warfare that was taking place in my mind. My flesh had taken over my spirit. My flesh controlled my spirit, instead of my spirit controlling my flesh. As a Christian, our flesh should be at the bottom of the totem pole, so to speak, but in my case, everything was all turned around.

# Valentines Day

Jumping ahead from the timeframe of this last story, I am going to tell you a remarkable story of God's timing! Many people might consider that it is sad, but I will explain how for me it demonstrated in another way that God was working on my behalf and drawing me close to Him. Because this happened when I was walking with Christ, and looking at things through the eyes of Christ, I had a very different perspective on this and all of the circumstances of my life.

In December of 1995, I returned to Texas to visit all of my family for the Christmas holidays. Scott and I were very close to having our divorce finalized. All that remained was for me to go to the courthouse to sign all of the papers; Scott did not have to be there because the divorce was uncontested. During my visit in Texas I called the lawyer in Florida to find out the date on which I would appear before the judge. My call was placed on hold while the lawyer's staff contacted the courthouse. As I waited, the Lord actually put these thoughts in my mind: "What if I have to see the judge for my final divorce decree on February 14, Valentine's Day? Lord, I know that is what is going to happen. The secretary is going to come back on the line and tell me to be in court on Valentine's Day. I know that You are preparing me for this." After several minutes, indeed, that is what happened. The secretary came back on the line exclaiming she was very sorry and that I was never going to believe the court date for finalizing my divorce. "Let me guess," I replied, "February 14." Surprised that I knew, she asserted that she had tried to get the court officer to change the date, but had been unsuccessful.

Are you thinking, how is this a God story? My God is so faithful, so kind, so compassionate. At this point in my life I was totally on fire for the Lord. For me, everything was about Jesus and for Jesus, though I still had my struggles. Valentine's Day, that day on which love is lavishly celebrated, seemed to me just the right day to finalize my divorce because I was trading in the tainted love of my marriage in order to be more immersed in the perfect love of Jesus. I had been falling in love with Jesus all over again, and in a much stronger way than I ever dreamed possible. I was now truly aware that He loved me deeply. That He was the lover of my soul. I was sure He only had good plans for me and would never bring harm to me. I knew that He had chosen February

14, 1996, as the day I would celebrate returning to my *first love* (Him) as a single (unmarried) person.

*Nevertheless I have this against you, that you have left your first love. Remember therefore from where you have fallen; repent and do the first works, or else I will come to you quickly and remove your lampstand from its place-- unless you repent.* Revelation 2:4-5 *(NKJV)*

On February 14, 1996, I hired a babysitter to watch my girls. I went to the courthouse all by myself because I had no family in Florida. Standing before the judge alone, I raised my hand, and my marriage of ten years, ten months, and nineteen days was dissolved. But I wasn't really alone; my Savior was present and preserving me the entire time. Comforted by Him, I headed to a familiar bench on a small cliff overlooking the ocean in Deerfield Beach. I had been there often to pray and seek the Lord. On this day, I prayed and cried, and Jesus held me in His arms. Then we, Jesus and I, went out to eat at a Chinese restaurant and spent the entire day together. I was on a date (something I actually do quite often now) with my Maker, my heavenly husband.

*For your Maker is your husband, the LORD of hosts is His name; and your Redeemer is the Holy One of Israel; he is called the God of the whole earth. For the LORD has called you like a woman forsaken and grieved in spirit, like a youthful wife when you were refused," says your God. "For a mere moment I have forsaken you, but with great mercies I will gather you. With a little wrath I hid My face from you for a moment; but with everlasting kindness I will have mercy on you," says the LORD, your Redeemer.* Isaiah 54:5-8 *(NKJV)*

Valentine's Day 1996 is a day that I will never forget because of Christ's great love for me. Yes, God does hate divorce, but He loves me more, and He did not want me to continue in sexual sin with my husband. God permits divorce when there is adultery involved, but I believe that He still hates divorce, even under those conditions. I was not strong enough as a Christian, at that time, to stay in that marriage and resist all of that sexual sin. I had to remove myself from it completely and begin rebuilding my relationship with Jesus Christ. Do I think my divorce was a sin? Actually, I do, because I now know that nothing is impossible with God; it's completely in His power to heal a broken marriage. The Lord has forgiven me for my sins and all of my days were ordained for me before even one of them came to be. Though the Lord knew I was going to divorce Scott and He knew the whole evil path that I would choose to take, He still hung on the Cross for me. He has always loved me, and always will, no matter what. During that time in my life, He picked me up as a helpless child, and He taught me how to crawl again, to walk again, and, finally, to run again, with reckless abandon, for the glory of His name!

So, my friend, my divorce on Valentine's Day is actually a God story to me. Every February 14 since then has a precious meaning and memory for me. It's a very special day between me and the Lord. He speaks to me on that day. I trust Him more than ever on that day. It is truly a day of love to me that comes from above.

# Rock Bottom

This next story is the most difficult for me to relate to you. This series of events brought me, at last, back to the Lord. Finally, I hit the proverbial "rock bottom."

I would rather tell you that I kissed ten women (which I didn't) than tell you about my efforts to seduce a married man. In my opinion, this is about the worst thing that a woman could ever do.

The tears are streaming down my face now as I begin to recount this tale. How could I have done this?! I am still so very sorry about this episode. Thinking about it reminds me how thankful I am that God continued to love me despite this event, and reminds me that he sent His son to die so I could be washed clean of this sin, and all my sins, *forever.* I am so thankful God did not give up on me, that he did not leave me in the pit that I was in at the time of this experience. In His infinite compassion, He did not just look at what I was doing, but He saw me through the eyes of Christ. Yes, for this moment in my past, I was a Proverbs 7 woman, but I am not that woman anymore. I am a new creation in Christ.

Remember the neighbor I told you about before--the married man who gazed at me through the fence in my backyard and also through my kitchen window? I believe that the Lord used this man to bring me to my knees spiritually. Because of what I saw, and what I sensed in my spirit, I believe that this man and his wife were Christians. It appeared that they attended church on Sunday mornings, yet obviously he was being unfaithful to his wife on one level because he was lusting after me. (If I, as a married person, even look at someone in lust, according to Jesus I am committing adultery. And if a single person gazes on another with lust, he or she is committing fornication, or sex outside of marriage, which is also a sin.)

*"You have heard that it was said to those of old, 'You shall not commit adultery.'* *"But I say to you that whoever looks at a woman to lust for her has already committed adultery with her in his heart."* Matthew 5:27-28 *(NKJV)*

One evening I was washing dishes and it was very late, probably after midnight. Since I did not have an automatic dishwasher, I was there for a while, washing all the dishes by hand. Looking up, I could see that my neighbor was in his kitchen staring through his window at me. His kitchen was dark but I could see he was there because a hall light was lit behind him. My husband was sitting at our kitchen table talking with me. Scornfully I remarked to Scott that this man was looking at me at that very moment. I had never lusted for my neighbor; I suppose that I was so busy with sexual sin elsewhere that I had never given much thought to this man. Scott was very amused, laughing out loud about how this guy gawked at me all the time. Suddenly, I saw his wife walk up from behind him and begin to yell at him. All the way from his house to ours, Scott and I could hear her yelling. Swiftly the curtains in their kitchen were drawn shut, and the yelling continued until finally, it stopped and all was quiet.

Considering that both Scott and I had committed adultery not long before this event, you would think that I would have felt bad for my neighbors, but I didn't. From what I remember, my thought was, "It serves that man right. He should not be looking at me. It's not my fault. I have not initiated anything with him at all."

But the next day, I did initiate something. I kept thinking about how many times I caught him staring at me and countless times he had come home at lunchtime to look at me through his backyard fence. I did not know him and really did not know anything about him at all except that I had discovered where he worked. Once while jogging I had seen him drive into his workplace parking lot, which was close to our neighborhood. That made it easy for me, and I called him up at his workplace.

Essentially, with a haughty tone, I demanded, "So what are you doing? Why are you looking at me all of the time? I always see you looking at me. Is something going to happen between us or do you think that you are just going to keep staring at me? If we are not going to have sex then I want you to stop looking at me. So, what's it going to be?"

Even as I type this I am amazed at the audacity I showed in my sexual sin. I was on a path of vengeance against my husband, and whoever crossed my path, I was going to take down. Though I had no desire for him, the behavior of this married man made me angry. I share these details to give you an understanding of just how messed up my mind was as a result of my steady descent into more and viler sexual sin. I just didn't care about anyone or who might get hurt as the result of my actions. I thought my neighbor's wife was a fool, just as I had been regarding my husband. I had been so blind-sided and devastated by my husband's infidelity that I had come to see myself as a complete and utter fool. Having been betrayed by my husband who I had trusted completely, I now felt that *no man* could be trusted. From my very disturbed perspective, I thought any man would do anything to have sex with a beautiful woman and I was sure he would accept my brazen offer.

I still marvel that I made that phone call and said those words, but I did. It shocks me that I was a Proverbs 7 immoral woman. I went after a married man and I went after him hard. No mincing words on my part. I went straight for the kill. The truth is, it didn't even seem like me when I picked up the phone and dialed the number that day; and everything about the way I spoke to him was out of character for me. Sin had completely taken over me. I was not possessed by a demon, but I was possessed by my sin. By this time I had become possessed by the power of sin; it controlled every part of me; my mind, my flesh, and the heart of my soul which had become darkened by sexual immorality.

And how did a small-town, sweet, loving Christian girl become an immoral woman, possessed by sexual sin? It started by me having immoral sex with my husband. I had been having immoral sex for several years by this time. Though I never could have imagined this would happen (and still, I can hardly believe that it did happen), it makes perfect sense. My downward spiral of sin illustrates the teaching of scripture. Sin grows. Sin devours. Sin destroys. Sin kills.

Praise the Lord that this man was a Christian! Praise the Lord that even though my neighbor had been dabbling with sin, obviously contemplating it in his mind, at that moment he turned from his sin. After my shameless invitation to adultery, he calmly, flatly refused me. "Nothing is going to happen between us," he declared, and hung up the phone. I will never forget that very moment. I dropped to my knees and I began sobbing deeply. I could not stop crying and it seemed that I cried for hours. As the flow of tears softened my hardened, wicked heart, I asked the Lord, right then and there, to please forgive me of my sins. Now that I wanted Him back in my life, I felt His presence immediately. As I cried and prayed and prayed and cried, Jesus held me in His arms and comforted me with His infinite love. He held me for hours. And at last, I knew I was back, close again to my Savior! He had been there, waiting for me to return to Him, the entire time.

At the time this happened, Scott and I were living partially separated. He would stay at our house sometimes but other times he stayed in a small recreational vehicle we owned. I called him on the phone and asked him to come home. I confessed my failed attempt to seduce our neighbor by calling him at his workplace, and I related to Scott how I had rededicated my life to the Lord. I wanted him to move back to our home permanently, so that we could start fresh in the Lord together.

Scott returned home very quickly and within minutes of his return there was a knock at our door. The police were there, responding to a complaint by my neighbor that I had harassed him at work. No charges were being pressed the policeman explained; it was just a complaint. Scott recounted the chain of events that had taken place the night before to the policeman, who found it all extremely amusing. In the end, he practically apologized that he had to issue the complaint against me since I had only called the neighbor that one time. Wow, what a day I had just had: Attempted to seduce a married man, rededicated my life to the Lord, asked my husband to move back home, and was visited by the police for the first time in my life. Not a dull moment, that's for sure!

In writing this book and sharing all these scandalous details of my past, I know that I am opening up a door for others to look at me with great judgment. I know that some may whisper unkind or untrue remarks about me, in my hometown, in my extended family, in my church, and at my workplace. I can withstand the whispered comments of others, because I have already endured the greatest whisperer of all, the accuser of the brethren, our immortal enemy. There were plenty of times he has haunted me, speaking lies and accusations to me when I was alone. I have overcome and beaten the enemy in the dark of the night, because I refuse to listen to his lies. I will shout in the dark of the night, and I will shout in the light of the day that my Savior has changed my life and that my Savior can change your life! I will tolerate the whispers of others with the hope that you, my dear friend, may see the freedom that you can have from your past, in Christ Jesus.

## Glorious Confession

This God story actually occurred about four months after I rededicated my life to the Lord. Scott and I were separated again because the sexual issues were so severe; I needed time to heal alone. I was rebuilding my relationship with the Lord, and spiritually I was growing very rapidly. With His infinite wisdom, God had placed me in a fantastic non-denominational Bible-teaching church in Ft. Lauderdale, and I was totally on fire for Jesus Christ!

I had repented of my sins, yet there was something that I knew I needed to do. I had to look into the eyes of the wife of the man I had tried to seduce, and apologize to her. So I got in my car, drove around the block to my neighbor's house, and knocked on the door, which she opened as I introduced myself. Graciously, she listened to me as I stood in her doorway. I communicated to her about my life, about the sexual sin in my marriage, about how perverted my mind had become. I confessed to her about my phone call to her husband and recounted how he had responded to me, remaining faithful to her. (The police who visited to deliver the complaint against me had previously told me the neighbor's wife was aware of what had occurred.) I was gently crying as I verbalized my apology to her, all the while looking directly in her eyes. I also shared with her about my relationship with Jesus and how my life was changing in Him. Expressing deepest sorrow for what I had done, I asked for her forgiveness. Though she was obviously uncomfortable, she was very kind to me.

Even though I know this was the right thing to do, it is incredible to me that I actually did it. Jesus called me to do it, and I know it was He who granted me the courage to look this woman in the eyes and apologize. I already knew that I was truly forgiven in Christ, but I had sinned against this woman, against her marriage, and I felt I had to tell her face to face that I was sorry and that Jesus had changed me. That is what is so amazing about our Jesus! It was His strength that spoke through me to this woman.

*"Therefore if you bring your gift to the altar, and there remember that your brother has something against you, leave your gift there before the altar, and go your way. First be reconciled to your brother, and then come and offer your gift."* Matthew 5:23-24 *(NKJV)*

*Pursue peace with all people, and holiness, without which no one will see the Lord.* Hebrews 12:14 *(NKJV)*

I am so glad that Jesus called me and equipped me to deliver that apology. At the time, I just knew that I had to tell her that I had turned from my sin, that I had re-surrendered my life to the Lord, and that I was a new creation in Christ. Somehow, I am quite certain, Jesus used the moments that I spent with her that day to bring glory to Himself. I trust that it was uplifting to her faith to hear about what Jesus had done for me.

Fall more in love with Jesus TODAY!

# FIVE
## Upward Climb

I would love to tell you that from the moment I rededicated my life to the Lord, I walked faithfully with the Lord. Unfortunately, that is not the case. I messed up badly one more time. In my opinion, it was actually the worst sin that I committed. We humans like to categorize sin, thinking some are worse than others, but in God's eyes, sin is sin. I love that about Him! There is only one unforgivable sin and that is denying Jesus Christ as the Son of God.

*Therefore I say to you, every sin and blasphemy will be forgiven men, but the blasphemy against the Spirit will not be forgiven men.* Matthew 12:31 *(NKJV)*

## Roadblocks from the Lord

After rededicating my life to the Lord I started attending church regularly with a sincere desire to get my life back in step with the Lord. But my mind was so corrupt from my steady diet of sinful behaviors that I soon came to realize I would need to make some very drastic changes. Instead of going to church and easily leaving behind my sinful ways, I learned that I was going to have to take measured steps in order to win the battle against the sin that was so deeply entrenched in my life.

Remember the policeman I befriended while attending classes to become a personal trainer? Before I had rededicated my life to the Lord, but during the time he was separated from his wife and Scott and I were separated, he and I had initiated a sexual relationship, though we had never had sexual intercourse. In my worldly view, since we were both separated, it was okay to do this.

What I now know is that it certainly is not okay. I was still married and he was still married. In God's eyes, and His is the most important view of all, no matter how long a couple may have been separated, they are still married, "one flesh." A married person should never be dating someone else and a married person should never be sexually active with someone else. What I was doing was very wrong, immoral, and specifically in violation of the Ten Commandments. It does not matter even if you are in the process of filing for divorce, you are still married and are obligated to remain faithful, sexually and otherwise. The Lord honors obedience and observing this warning is being obedient. Until the day that the divorce paper is signed by the judge, you are still married. God can heal. God can restore. God can do the impossible, even after that divorce paper is signed. I have a story which illustrates those statements and I will share it with you later.

After rededicating my life to the Lord, I informed the cop that I was going to stop meeting with him before class, which is the time we had had to be alone together. When about six weeks had passed he called me on the phone, asking that I meet him at a motel. Though in the past he had been reluctant, now he vowed he wanted to have sex with me, just this once. Though he knew that I had turned away from this type of lifestyle, he argued that since we had invested so much time together, we really should meet. (Remember, Scott had moved back in with me on the day that I pledged my life back to the Lord.)

Upon hanging up the phone, the debate in my mind began. "Meet him at the motel. You have been waiting for this for months. You can do this one last thing, and then get serious with the Lord." And the other voice in my head said, "No. You can't do this. Just stop now!" But then I would think, "Just this one last time. Just meet him this one last time." Well, I made up my mind: I was going to go and have sex with the cop and then I was going to start walking strong with the Lord. That was the decision that I made, and I felt sure that is what I was going to do.

Before I continue to tell you this part of my story, I would like to take a few minutes to talk about the enemy. I was a Christian and a Christian can never be possessed by a demon, inside of their flesh. Here is the scripture that backs up my belief on that:

*You are of God, little children, and have overcome them, because He who is in you is greater than he who is in the world.* I John 4:4 *(NKJV)*

Jesus lived inside of me and that means that a demon could not also live inside of me. Jesus protects me from that ever happening but that does not mean that a demon cannot "oppress" a Christian. Though I didn't realize it, at this time I was demon-oppressed. I am explaining this because although this next scripture speaks of being demon possessed and that does not exactly describe my condition, the principal is true of those who are demon-oppressed also.

*"When an unclean spirit goes out of a man, he goes through dry places, seeking rest, and finds none. Then he says, 'I will return to my house from which I came.' And when he comes, he finds it empty, swept, and put in order. Then he goes and takes with him seven other spirits more wicked than himself, and they enter and dwell there; and the last state of that man is worse than the first. So shall it also be with this wicked generation."* Matthew 12:43-45 *(NKJV)*

With that teaching in mind, let me explain what I believe happened to me. I was heavily oppressed by the demonic world, and then I rededicated my life to the Lord and started going to church. I was sweeping my house clean, so to speak, but I had not yet begun to take steps to fight against the sin in my life. Scott and I were back together but still struggling with our ungodly sexual relationship. I was still watching pornography occasionally and I still had a couple of sexual devices I used at times. I was not yet knowledgeable about exactly what had taken place in my spiritual life, nor about what was taking place in the spiritual realm around me. Until you learn of something, you are ignorant of it, because you honestly do not know it. That is to say, I honestly had no understanding that when I rededicated my life to the Lord I was going to have to take a part in my own sanctification. I didn't realize how deep my downward spiral of sexual sin had taken me, so I also could not comprehend the great climb that I would need to make to get out of that pit.

Having given my life back to the Lord and swept my house clean, the spiritual world was taking notice of me. Though I had made a few godly changes in my life the enemy was watching and could observe that I was still incredibly weak in my spirit. The last thing that the enemy wants is for a Christian to get strong in the Lord. A lost person does not scare the enemy, since that lost person belongs to the enemy. It is an on-fire Christian who scares the enemy to death! The enemy desires to bring death to your life, and when you are not walking with the Lord, he is accomplishing that task. It is when you are walking with the Lord that you are actually bringing harm to the enemy. Indeed, the devoted, God-centered, spirit-filled Christian scares the enemy to death! We have a choice in so many areas of our life. So, what's it going to be my friend? *Your* destruction, or the death of the enemy? It's really your choice. The enemy was watching me clean house, to a certain extent, and he then came in for the kill.

Everything we do reflects a choice we have made. We always think about things in our minds before we willfully do them. Though I had persistently refused to do the things my husband had pressured me to do, in the end, I decided to do them with him--it was my choice. I thought about them and then I chose to do them. You must accept that each of us *decides* if she is going to walk in sin or going to walk with God. It really is our own choice, but when we do choose to walk with God, we don't do that in *our own strength*. It is His strength that keeps us walking with Him, when we allow Him to take over our lives. If we decide to walk in the ways of the world, the enemy is right there waiting to devour us.

As you have read in the preceding pages, I committed a lot of sins. But things progressed much differently when I decided to commit this sin. Remember, I had made a new pledge of faith to the Lord. Knowing my heart, He knew that I was genuine about walking with Him but that I was also still extremely weak spiritually. Though I did not have the power in my spirit to resist this temptation, the Lord intervened in very supernatural ways. He put up numerous road blocks to stop me from committing this sin, because He loved me so much. In the midst of my wickedness, He showed me just how much He will do for His children when their hearts and spirits really want to follow Him. Only He really knows our hearts, and He knew that I really wanted to walk with Him. Listen to what He did for me--stand back and be amazed!

These "roadblocks," which I am calling instead sin blocks, gave me opportunities to avoid the sin that ensnared me. Though I didn't take advantage of them in the way God wanted me to, still when I looked back after the fact I could see a picture of the immeasurable, unconditional love that He has for me.

## Sin Block #1

The cop and I were preparing to meet and about two weeks before our meeting date his wife moved back home with him. Although they had determined to try again to make their marriage work, he still wanted to meet with me. I could not believe the timing of this, but I had already purposed in my heart to commit this sin. I did hesitate, but chose to keep moving forward towards committing this sin.

## Sin Block #2

Now that his wife was back home, he claimed he could not pay for the motel room because she would wonder where that money had been spent. I would have to pay for the motel, he insisted. I could not believe it. Wow, this was not turning out to be much of a romance, but then again, it was never about romance at all, only about sex. I was in the same boat. I could not pay for the motel out of my checking account without having to answer to my husband about that money.

## Sin Block #3

I had a close friend in Texas who knew all about my screwed up life. A friend since high school, she believed that my years of sexual sin were something I had to go through because, I had had only one boyfriend in my lifetime and because I had married at such a young age. I felt comfortable telling her everything and I told her about this glitch in the meeting with the cop. Her response was, "No problem at all. I will mail you the money for the motel."

She did mail the money but days passed and I never received the money. Finally she called to let me know the money had been sent back to her home. The address on the envelope was correct but the post office had written on the envelope that it was not correct. Only God could do that!

## Sin Block #4

In the meantime, I had called a friend in another state and lied to her. I claimed I needed money for my personal training school and could she please wire it to my account, which she did. Are you thinking, "You rededicated your life to the Lord and you're acting like *this*?" Yes, and yes. God knew my heart. God knew my struggles. God knew the depth of my sin. He knew how far I had fallen and how incredibly weak I was. But that's not the end of his efforts to prevent me from committing this sin.

## Sin Block #5

The money arrived in my account and for some reason the bank called my husband to inform him of this transaction. Naturally he questioned me about the money, and I lied to him. Actually, I don't even remember what I told him, but whatever it was, he believed me.

So again, I avoided yet another opportunity to back down from committing adultery. I had committed adultery with a single guy but I had not yet committed adultery with a married man, even though I had tried once before with my neighbor. I believe it was the demon-oppression that caused me to be so relentless. I pushed through all these interferences with the arrangements for the meeting with the cop. See what God did next.

## Sin Block #6

I worked out on a regular basis and at this time I was in the best shape of my life. I had only 11% body fat and for a woman that is remarkable, a very tough goal to reach. I would do pull ups in my backyard using a very large branch on one of my trees, and I did this frequently.

Three days before we were to meet at the motel I was working out in my backyard, doing my pull ups. I was pulling up on the branch when suddenly the branch split open and I crashed into the trunk of the tree. My chest slammed the trunk of that tree with tremendous speed and force. I was in severe pain and could barely breathe. Home alone and knowing our family had no health insurance, I neglected to call an ambulance, though I should have done so. I could have driven myself to the emergency room but I didn't do that either.

Nothing has ever hurt my physical body as much as that injury. When Scott came home that night and I explained to him what happened, he wanted me to go to the doctor. But because he had just received a cut in pay, and because of my foolishness, I refused to go. I could tell that I had fractured my sternum and I thought that there was nothing that a doctor could do about that type of fracture. I needed pain medication but I do have a very high tolerance for pain, so I just accepted that I would deal with the physical pain. If you had touched my chest with one finger and applied pressure, I would have been screaming in pain. But do you think I called off my meeting with the cop at the motel? No, I pressed forward into committing adultery as planned; I was determined not to let God stop me.

You see, I realized exactly what was going on by this time. In my past sins, I had not been attempting to walk with God. I had decided to turn my back on the Lord, and He was patiently waiting for me to turn around and look back into His eyes. Now that I had turned back to Him, everything had changed. This time, as I stepped out into this sin, things were much different. God began to take major action to prevent His child from hurting herself. He put up roadblock after roadblock, or sin block after sin block.

We, as parents, tell our children to be careful. We tell them, "Don't touch that or else you will get burned." We put safety latches on cabinets to prevent our children from reaching for poisons, and we put up safety rails to keep our children from falling down the stairs. Just as we take strategic measures to keep our children from getting hurt, our Father in heaven does the same for His children. He went to extremes to protect me, even allowing me to be in severe physical pain, in order to prevent me from spiritual pain. I could not be more certain that it was no accident or coincidence that the tree branch split open when it did. I had been doing pull ups on it for months and knew it was a very strong branch. God allowed that branch to break to show me the lengths that He would go to in order to persuade me to turn from my sin. He knew all along that I was not going to listen, but believe me, I was taking note of what He was doing. I did receive the message He was sending me, though I did not do what He wanted me to do.

# Sin Block #7

The day finally arrived and it was time for me to go to commit my sin. I was so pathetic and so stubborn. My plan was that I would just go to commit this sin this one last time and then I would walk with God! By this time I was getting mad at God for trying to stop me. "Just leave me alone, God," I thought. "Seriously, what is up with all of this? It's not that big of a deal. I have been in sexual sin for years now. Just let me do this one last thing."

On the way, I stopped at a convenience store to get a pack of gum and when I got back in my car it would not start. Can you believe this?! God is so faithful, but I just spit at His faithfulness. I sat there for a few minutes and then tried starting it again. After hesitating, the car started up.

I arrived at the motel first, paid for the room, and waited for the cop to arrive. I remember thinking, as I sat there, "I cannot believe I am going through with this." I could not believe that I was going to commit adultery against my husband and that I was going to commit adultery with a married man. I wanted to run out of that motel right then, but I didn't. Instead, I calmly waited for the chance to commit the sin.

He arrived and we had sex, the worst sexual experience of my entire life. There was no pleasure whatsoever, no satisfaction whatsoever, and I was in incredible pain because of my fractured sternum. I was a dog returning to my own vomit. Would you eat vomit? Sounds like a very stupid question, but that is exactly what we are doing when we walk right back into our sin. Whether it's sex, drugs, alcohol, bitterness, pride, envy, unforgiveness, or something else, it's all vomit, and we are choosing to eat it. As disgusting as that sounds, it is truth!

*As a dog returns to his own vomit, so a fool repeats his folly.* Proverbs 26:11 *(NKJV)*

*For if, after they have escaped the pollutions of the world through the knowledge of the Lord and Savior Jesus Christ, they are again entangled in them and overcome, the latter end is worse for them than the beginning. For it would have been better for them not to have known the way of righteousness, than having known it, to turn from the holy commandment delivered to them. But it has happened to them according to the true proverb: "A dog returns to his own vomit,"* and, *"a sow, having washed, to her wallowing in the mire."* 2 Peter 2:20-22 *(NKJV)*

We finished what we planned to do and it was time for me to leave. I have never felt so empty in my whole life. He walked me out to my car and it would not start again. I looked up to the sky, and I said aloud to the Lord, "Leave me the 'F' alone!" But I did not say the letter F, I said "the F word" to Almighty God. I really did. How dare me! Who did I think I was? How could I have done that?

In my pain, in my emptiness, in my hopelessness, I cursed at my Lord. And you know what He was doing? He was crying for me. He felt my pain. He knew my frustration as I was trying to find some sort of satisfaction in this very empty world, trying to fill this monstrous void that was in my heart. He knew that I didn't really mean what I had just said.

I believe that His thoughts toward me that day were, "You are almost there, My precious daughter. You are so close. Don't give up on Me. Don't let go of My hand. You can do this. Choose Me. I will satisfy you in ways that you never dreamed possible. I will fill that void. I will take away that pain that you are carrying around deep within your soul. I will stop at nothing to have you. I will never leave you or forsake you. I don't care how many times you spit in My face, you can never run too far. I am always here for you. Come, My beloved daughter, and allow Me to take away all of this hurt. You are already glorified in My eyes. You are precious in My sight. Let Me show you what I have already done for you. You already hold the victory because you are mine."

As I cursed at my Lord, the pain from within came pouring out. We walked back into the motel room because we had to figure out what I was going to do. He told me that he had to leave very soon and he was sorry my car wouldn't start. Angry and annoyed, I ranted, "You are just going to leave me here? What am I going to do? My car won't start. I can't call my husband!" He advised me to call a tow truck which would come and jump my car to get it started again. I told him that I didn't have any money at all with me. I had already paid for the motel, but he maintained that though he was sorry, he couldn't pay the expense of the tow truck because his wife would question him about the money.

Overcome and feeling completely worthless, I started crying. Suddenly I realized that I was just a piece of trash to this man. I had already known that sex doesn't mean much, but I realized at that very moment just how little sex really meant. Despising him, I insisted that he had to pay for the tow truck. He didn't care about "Stacey" at all, but at last he took out his wallet and gave me fifty dollars for the tow truck; and then he left the motel.

As I sat alone waiting for the tow truck, all of the roadblocks, the sin blocks, came flashing back to my memory. I recognized the many marvelous things God had done trying to prevent me from having to live through that evening. I realized how intimately the Lord's hand was on my life, and how real and how personal the Lord really is. Not just some supreme being way up high in the sky, He is right here with me and He cares about me. He really does not want me to live in sin and will do whatever it takes to prevent His daughter from walking down the wrong path. He showed Himself to me in a much different way than I had ever known Him before, but not because He was acting any differently. It was because my heart was responding differently.

At age fifteen I knew that I needed Him for my salvation, to save me from hell. But finally, at age twenty-seven, I realized that I needed Him to help me walk through this life, each day. I had come to understand that I wasn't going to wait until eternity to be with my Savior; instead He would be walking with me in this world, in the here and now.

I finally realized that I was not alone in that motel room. My Savior had been there the whole time, even during the adultery. He knew His lost sheep was on her way back home and He would not leave my side, even for one second. He looked on my sin that night, as I was committing it, but it was no surprise to Him at all. You want to know why? He had already looked on my sin two thousand years earlier. He had already lived through that moment with me as He hung on the Cross. When He was being pierced with those nails, He was saying my name, while looking at all of my sins. And here's the craziest thing about the Cross— He took my sins off of me and placed them upon Himself. Jesus Christ placed my adultery upon His own flesh. He placed all of my sexual immorality upon Himself as He hung on that Cross for my sins; as He hung on that Cross for the sins of the whole entire world.

*For He made Him who knew no sin to be sin for us, that we might become the righteousness of God in Him.* 2 Corinthians 5:21 *(NKJV)*

In that motel room, God did not see a worthless piece of trash, or even a sexually immoral woman or an adulteress. Instead, God saw me, His daughter, covered in the blood of Jesus Christ His Son. From the top of my head to the tips of my toes, I was drenched in the blood of Jesus Christ.

The upward climb back to my Lord had truly begun on the day that I had rededicated, even though I messed up miserably that night. That night's sin was different than the past sexual sins because I had placed my heart back into His hands about a month earlier. His presence surrounded me and He was in hot pursuit to gain my attention.

*And you have forgotten the exhortation which speaks to you as to sons: "My son, do not despise the chastening of the Lord, nor be discouraged when you are rebuked by Him; For whom the Lord loves He chastens, and scourges every son whom He receives." If you endure chastening, God deals with you as with sons; for what son is there whom a father does not chasten? But if you are without chastening, of which all have become partakers, then you are illegitimate and not sons. Furthermore, we have had human fathers who corrected us, and we paid them respect. Shall we not much more readily be in subjection to the Father of spirits and live? For they indeed for a few days chastened us as seemed best to them, but He for our profit, that we may be partakers of His holiness. Now no chastening seems to be joyful for the present, but painful; nevertheless, afterward it yields the peaceable fruit of righteousness to those who have been trained by it.* Hebrews 12:5-11 *(NKJV)*

At last the tow truck came and the mechanic started my vehicle with jumper cables. I don't remember what lie I had given my husband about where I was going, but I drove home feeling completely defeated, and went straight to bed. The next morning I woke up and I never looked back. I knew that the Lord really did love me unconditionally, and I needed to be loved.

## Alive and Active

Finally I realized that I was going to have to make some material changes in my life, or else I would remain stuck in my world of spiritual sin. I began to read the Word of God for five minutes a day. No, I'm not kidding. That may sound like a miniscule change to you, but at that time I did not have a love for reading the Bible and I had to force myself to do that much. Probably more important than the five minutes was the attitude I brought to the Lord. I told Him, "Lord, I know that You are my only way out of this type of lifestyle. I know that all of the answers to life's problems are in Your Word. I know that *You* are my only answer. So, I am giving you this five minutes a day reading your Word, believing that You will change my life."

And so, because the Lord is faithful and loves us more than we can ever fathom, He responded to my request and my belief. Knowing I was truly and desperately searching for truth, He began to cause my life to change drastically, very quickly. My five-minutes-a-day quiet time with the Lord turned into ten minutes, and then my ten minutes turned into twenty minutes. I fell in love with the Word of God and before long I enjoyed spending an hour or more a day reading the Bible. I could hardly put it down, because God's Word became extremely exciting to me. And along with this love of the Word, I found a new excitement in living my life--an excitement that satisfied me beyond my wildest imagination.

Here's an example of what was taking place in my life, concerning the Word of God: I was reading the Bible one night out on my hammock, under the stars. I was feeling very frustrated because I was still having immoral thoughts and I was still having self sex. I really wanted to be sexually pure, but the corrupt things that I did not want to do, I did still do. Feeling frustrated and discouraged, I called my church and left a message on the answering machine for my pastor to call me. About 2,500 people attended my church at that time, but I just knew Pastor Bob would call me back. I sensed that he was just that type of a pastor. I left the message and then I continued to read God's Word. Though I had read the Bible as a teenager, I had not read it much in a very long time, and most of it remained unfamiliar to me.

By what I now know was God's divine guidance, I was reading in the book of Romans. I had started at the beginning of that book and when I came to Romans 7, I was astonished to find that the thoughts that had been so frustrating to me were right there on the page, expressed by Paul, the writer of Romans! I leapt from the hammock, and, jumping up and down, I cried out to the Lord, "I can't believe this! I never imagined that you know how I am feeling! It's incredible that You are talking about this! This is so incredible!" I called my church again and left another message. "Pastor Bob, you do not have to call me now," I exclaimed excitedly. "All of my questions were just answered in Romans 7! This is incredible! God's Word is incredible! Thank you! Bye!"

Here is the section of scripture that precisely echoed my thoughts that evening:

*For we know that the law is spiritual, but I am carnal, sold under sin. For what I am doing, I do not understand. For what I will to do, that I do not practice; but what I hate, that I do. If, then, I do what I will not to do, I agree with the law that it is good. But now, it is no longer I who do it, but sin that dwells in me. For I know that in me (that is, in my flesh) nothing good dwells; for to will is present with me, but how to perform what is good I do not find. For the good that I will to do, I do not do; but the evil I will not to do, that I practice. Now if I do what I will not to do, it is no longer I who do it, but sin that dwells in me. I find then a law, that evil is present with me, the one who wills to do good. For I delight in the law of God according to the inward man. But I see another law in my members, warring against the law of my mind, and bringing me into captivity to the law of sin which is in my members. O wretched man that I am! Who will deliver me from this body of death? I thank God-- through Jesus Christ our Lord! So then, with the mind I myself serve the law of God, but with the flesh the law of sin.* Romans 7:14-25 *(NKJV)*

I was astounded that God's Word described exactly what I was going through. Excited and comforted, I reflected on what this passage was telling me about God: He *really* knows me, I thought, and He understands! He did not leave me helpless and hopeless. With this new discovery, I felt encouraged to devour God's Word even more intensely. I began to realize that my life could change, and indeed, it was changing!

At my request, Scott had moved out again, for what turned out to be the final time. There were so many things I needed to work through emotionally: the adultery he committed; the adulteries that I committed; the fantasies, the pornography, the sexual devices, the men, the women. As you can clearly see from what I have shared, I was one messed up woman, and I believed I needed a time of separation in order to focus on my Savior, to allow Him to heal my mind and my life.

Twice a week I was in church, meeting other on-fire Christians and learning to worship with all my heart. Rather than singing a few hymns in between announcements and prayers, this church had a focused time of worship for about the first thirty minutes of the service. Though I had never experienced that in all my years of attending church, it really ministered to me. Thirty minutes of uninterrupted worship! God knew this was what I needed; He was teaching me to praise my Savior; to truly worship Jesus.

Much about this church was new and surprising to me. I didn't feel dirty or judged there, partly because it seemed this church was full of ex-drug addicts, ex-alcoholics, ex-strippers, ex-homosexuals. Yet I noticed there were also plenty of folks who came to church still bound up in their sins. I observed these struggling sinners, desiring to be set free, offering up praise and worship to the Lord, and thirstily soaking up the wisdom of God that was being preached from the pulpit. Recognizing that I was in this category of struggling sinners, I knew I had found my spiritual home for this season of my life. It was one of the greatest times in my life, even though I still had very deep-rooted pain. I was seeking my Savior, and He was rebuilding me one day at a time.

Within about three months of starting this period of growth in the Lord I found myself faced with two decisions. Not realizing how detrimental it was for me to continue associations with people from my sinful past, I had kept in touch with Mark (Scott's friend in South Beach) and now he had invited me to a party that would be really spectacular, he claimed, with Hollywood celebrities and other immensely wealthy people. Honestly, it was a great temptation for me.

Though my spirit was growing stronger, my flesh was still very much alive. However, I had begun to really fear the Lord, in a reverent way. I remembered all of the ways the Lord had tried to prevent me from committing adultery. I realized God was very intent upon keeping me on His straight and narrow path. Still, I was in the best shape of my life and newly-separated from my husband; I was not as naïve as I had been and had developed approaches for getting what I wanted. Thoughtfully, I took the time to consider in my mind what was likely to happen if I went to this party. I knew it was extremely unlikely that the people I met there would be people who were walking with God. Recognizing that I would be putting myself in danger spiritually, and appreciating that I was not yet strong enough to resist that type of temptation if I went, I made the decision not to go. Praise God I said no! In the end, I felt pleased that I seemed to be increasing in wisdom and strength from the Lord.

About a month later another temptation arose. My personal trainer, who was a good friend of mine but not a Christian, had a boyfriend who had competed successfully in bodybuilding contests. Through friends of his, I was offered a position with a bodybuilding magazine and invited to move to California. Since I was in great shape, *and* the mom of four beautiful daughters, the magazine staff saw a great marketing opportunity in using photos of the five of us in the magazine. Although it seemed like a dream-come-true job for a single mom with no college education, I carefully imagined what might happen if I took this job and moved to California. I believed I would make good money and meet a lot of worldly men, and I feared I would not be strong enough to resist the temptations of this world. In addition, I realized that what my heart really wanted, the only thing that my heart wanted at this point in my life, was for my Jesus to take care of me, love me, and teach me how to be a strong and Godly woman. I desired desperately to be a Godly woman. So I declined the offer, without regret. Praise God I was able to see and do what God wanted me to do!

Slowly my sinful flesh was losing its control over my life and my spirit was rapidly growing. I began to have a joy that I had never experienced before. I was falling so deeply in love with my Savior and He was cleansing me from within.

## A New Creation

Now I want to slow down to tell you my God story about being baptized. It was June 24, 1995, and I had decided to participate in a baptism that the pastors and elders of my church were conducting at a park. This would be the second time I would be baptized and though I knew that the first time was enough, since I had traveled down such a dark path as a Christian I really desired to be baptized again. On the day of the baptism I had just fasted for three days. This was the first time in my life that I ever fasted, taking only water for three days. I felt that the Lord had led me to design a special plan for my baptism and it was important to me that I follow the plan precisely: After a three day fast, I would walk into the water, be immersed in the water, then brought back up to a new life. Then I would walk out of the water and take a bite of bread (in this case a bagel), symbolic of the bread of life. I really enjoy making unique, symbolic plans such as this with my Lord. My relationship with Him is the most exciting part of my life and this is one way I celebrate that with Him. Since He died and rose on the third day, I wanted to fast for three days, and then be raised out of the water to my new life in Him.

When I rededicated my life to the Lord a few months prior to this baptism, I had written my pastor a very long letter, describing much of what had happened in my life concerning my marriage and my sexual sins. I signed the letter with my first name, Stacey, but since there were more than two thousand people attending the church at that time, and because I had never spoken to Pastor Bob face-to-face, I believed he would have no idea who I was. Our church was in a season of very rapid growth, with many people making new professions of faith at each service, every weekend. Baptism events were held several times each year, and typically well over a hundred people would be baptized. Therefore Pastor Bob was joined by many other pastors and elders who, in teams of two, performed the baptisms. And even though Pastor Bob did not know me, I *really* wanted for him to be the one to baptize me that day.

Why? Because the Lord had used Pastor Bob so powerfully in my life. His transparency in the pulpit and His dedication to preaching directly from the Bible were tools the Lord used during this season to help me grow up in the knowledge and understanding of the Lord. As I stood on the water's edge, I prayed, "Please Lord, I want Pastor Bob to be the one who baptizes me, but I realize he is only a man. I am not going to move to get in the line to be baptized by Pastor Bob, but if Pastor Bob walks out in the water, directly in front of me, then and only then, I will know You have arranged for him to be the one who baptizes me."

Opening my eyes after I prayed, I watched as the twenty-some men took their places in the water to begin baptizing. Directly across from me was Pastor Bob! I was so pleased. God knew this was important to me and He divinely arranged for it to happen. As I walked out to Pastor Bob, waist-deep in the water, I began to meditate on what was taking place spiritually. I was "doing" Romans 6. I was going to go down into the water in the likeness of Christ's death and I was going to come up into the newness of life. My sins were getting buried in that water on that very day. I was getting baptized into Christ's death.

*What shall we say then? Shall we continue in sin that grace may abound? Certainly not! How shall we who died to sin live any longer in it? Or do you not know that as many of us as were baptized into Christ Jesus were baptized into His death? Therefore we were buried with Him through baptism into death, that just as Christ was raised from the dead by the glory of the Father, even so we also should walk in newness of life. For if we have been united together in the likeness of His death, certainly we also shall be in the likeness of His resurrection.* Romans 6:1-5 *(NKJV)*

Pastor Bob began to speak to me and I was astonished, because I had never had a conversation with him before this moment. "I understand that you have compromised some in your Christian walk, Stacey," he said gently, "but the Lord has covered you in His blood. You have been backsliding but you have come back to the Lord. He loves you very much." He then dunked me in the water, and helped me back up, baptizing me in the name of the Father, the Son and the Holy Spirit. I walked out of the water and heard my then-favorite song being sung, *White As Snow*—another special gift from God to me. As I listened to the song and broke my three day fast by eating some of my bagel, I reveled in what was one of the most beautiful, precious moments of my entire life. I *knew* I was as white as snow, that my Savior did not see any of my sins.

As I thought about it later, I was truly amazed that Pastor Bob knew my name! (Our church was so large, and I had not yet made many friends there.) And I realized, based on the things he said to me, that he had connected me with the letter that I had sent him. How marvelous it was then, that, knowing of all the sins that I had confessed in the letter, he said to me, "I understand that you have compromised some." Compromised some?! Wow, what an understatement that was. But that was so much like the grace of God! My pastor knew all of my sins and yet he saw me with the eyes of Christ. The words he spoke to me were gracious because our God is very gracious. I realized that the words Pastor Bob spoke to me were really a message to me from the Lord, who I imagined would have phrased it, "You have compromised some My darling daughter." That message was a very great gift from the Lord, one I will never ever forget.

## CHRISTIAN FRIENDS

Though I was not divorced yet, my marriage was definitely moving in that direction. Once Scott moved out, our marriage relationship became quite unpleasant. Simply stated, he was very angry with me. But my life was beginning to change in very good ways. At my church, I began to make friends and spend time with them. In particular, I met a Christian guy named Brad.

I believe the Lord brought Brad into my life to teach me a lot of things. He was an on-fire Christian man who loved the Lord with his whole heart. As you might guess, I am a very open and honest person, and in keeping with my character I shared all of the events of my recent past life with Brad, very early in our friendship. With the thoughtfulness of an older brother, Brad cautioned me that I should not be so open with men initially. Instead of taking advantage of my naiveté, and because he loved the Lord, Brad taught me that *all* sex outside of marriage is sin. I was truly surprised, since I had always believed that petting and oral sex were okay for unmarried persons. Before I met Brad, I thought that as long as I didn't have sexual intercourse, I could do everything else and still be moral. Brad, gently but firmly, corrected me, using scripture to inform me of God's truth about sexual matters. (In a latter section of this book I will address this topic with scripture also.) This was a whole new way of thinking for me. I was a baby Christian and Brad was using God's word to teach me how to crawl.

Brad and I were becoming great friends, until we made the mistake of involving ourselves in passionate kissing and foreplay. Since we knew that this was sin for us, it became a big problem in our relationship. I know that the man is the stronger vessel, but this poor guy was coming up against a woman (me) who was a sex addict. At times, I did not behave as a virtuous Christian lady with him and I know I really pushed him to his limits. Sadly, one night, he was weak. The remarkable thing for me was seeing with my own eyes the repentance in this man regarding our actions. I was amazed at how distraught he was; he actually wept because of what we had done. At the time, I thought, "We barely did anything. What is up with all of this?" But Brad knew that we were not God's will for each other as a couple, and he was strong enough to stop short of having sexual intercourse with me. He was strong enough to be a true friend. Yes, we sinned by our sexual expression, but the Lord forgave us, and Brad was a tool that the Lord used in my life. I am thankful for all that I learned from Brad.

Though I often did sense the joy of the Lord, and I was making friends at my church, I was still hurting deeply and my heart remained far from healed. One afternoon, bowed down on my bedroom floor, I cried out to God in distress. My life was a wreck, I whined. I was getting a divorce and I had four little girls to take care of all on my own. I still lived in the same house across from the neighbor I had tried to seduce and though he was no longer staring at me, I hated having that daily reminder of my sin. I was still having self sex on a regular basis, though I knew I needed to stop that practice. I suppose I figured that since I wasn't having sex with men, or watching pornography, God would cut me some slack for keeping one sexual device. In fact, I was taking God's grace for granted, but I believe that He knew how weak I was, and He was pouring out His grace to me anyway. He knew that I was not yet using, or even aware of, all of the spiritual tools I needed in order to walk in complete victory. So there on the bedroom floor, feeling sorry for myself, I sobbed, "I feel like a little baby Lord. I feel so helpless. I need You to hold me. I need You to carry me. I need You to take care of me. I need You to love me. I am such a baby, Lord."

That evening I attended an Afterglow Service at our church. This was a small, informal service, with no prepared sermon to be delivered, at which we expected the Gifts of The Holy Spirit to be manifested. After a time of singing, in the reverent, worshipful stillness, a woman stood up and said that the Lord had just given her a message, which she had written down in order to share it with all of us who were there. "It is a message for someone in this room," she announced. "The Lord says to you, 'You are my little baby. I am holding you in My arms. I will always take care of you. I will carry you through this life. I will always help you. I love you so much. You are My little baby.'"

Stunned, I began to weep, and then I stood up and shared with the group the words I had prayed just hours before that service. This miraculous manifestation of the Holy Spirit served to impress upon me that this God of mine was a very personal God. It reinforced to me that this God of mine had a concrete plan for my life, and that He was truly MY GOD! Receiving this personal message from God demonstrated to me, once again, that God cared for me more deeply than I could possibly imagine. God and I made a very special connection that evening, and I can tell you that I have never felt alone since that night. The God of Abraham, Isaac, and Jacob spoke directly to me in a supernatural way. He made His presence known to me through the power of His Holy Spirit, spoken through another human being. His Spirit spoke life into my broken heart. My Father held me in His arms and brought healing to my shattered life. I was His baby and He was, and still is, my Abba Father.

Despite all of the dreadful sins that I committed, God never made me feel less than beautiful. He has never made me feel dirty or disgusting, even though to the human eye many of the things that I have done are repulsive. Through the eyes of Christ, I am beautiful. Through the eyes of Christ, you, my friend, are beautiful, no matter what sins you have committed. Do not listen to the lies of the enemy which try to convince you otherwise. You are precious in His sight. He is a gracious and merciful God. He loves you and He forgives you of your sins. It is the goodness of God that leads us to repentance.

*Or do you despise the riches of His goodness, forbearance, and longsuffering, not knowing that the goodness of God leads you to repentance?* Romans 2:4 *(NKJV)*

During those days, though I had repented of my sins, I still cried frequently. But I didn't cry because I feared I wasn't forgiven; I cried to release the mountain of hurt and pain inside of me. The Lord had begun the process of healing me immediately, but it was going to take some time. Dear reader, we need to make sure that we allow people to go through their own healing processes, in their own way and on God's schedule. We often want to rush those around us; trying to encourage them, saying, "Smile! Be happy!" But we need to realize that we are all different and that we heal in different ways. No one on the face of this earth will ever know exactly what I went through, or precisely what I experienced, because I am the only *me* who God made. And you are the only *you* who God made. He understands your pain. He is your Father and you are His child. No one can completely understand what *you* are going through, except Jesus Christ, because He sees every detail of your pain. He feels your pain. He went through your pain, as He hung on the Cross.

*Your hands have made me and fashioned me; give me understanding, that I may learn Your commandments.* Psalms 119:73 *(NKJV)*

I made a lot of Christian friends at my church and I was at church at every opportunity. If the doors were opened, I wanted to be there and I needed to be there. I had been swallowed up in the ways of the world and I knew that I needed to be immersed instead in the ways of my Lord. I knew that I needed to hear the Word of God as much as possible. With God's help, I had learned very quickly that the Word is alive and active and that it did have the power to change my life. My life, my heart and my mind were changing, right before my eyes. I was truly in awe of The Word!

*For the word of God is living and powerful, and sharper than any two-edged sword, piercing even to the division of soul and spirit, and of joints and marrow, and is a discerner of the thoughts and intents of the heart. And there is no creature hidden from His sight, but all things are naked and open to the eyes of Him to whom we must give account. Seeing then that we have a great High Priest who has passed through the heavens, Jesus the Son of God, let us hold fast our confession. For we do not have a High Priest who cannot sympathize with our weaknesses, but was in all points tempted as we are, yet without sin. Let us therefore come boldly to the throne of grace, that we may obtain mercy and find grace to help in time of need.* Hebrews 4:12-16 *(NKJV)*

The Lord used another man I met at church, James, greatly in my life. We became close friends and I even worked for him as his administrative assistant. Though we were definitely attracted to one another, we came to know that it was not God's will that we become a couple. I know that we each prayed about our relationship, and one thing God showed me was that James was very uncomfortable about becoming a stepfather to my four little girls, all under the age of nine. We spent a lot of time together, and my hurting heart began to fall in love with him. I didn't realize at that time that I was just setting myself up for more heartache. The good news is that at least we did not fall into sexual sin.

From my relationship with James, I gained some wisdom that I want to pass along to you in the form of advice: If you are falling in love with someone and you know that it is not God's will for you to marry that person, then you need to *end that relationship immediately*; as difficult as it may be. James was not looking for a committed relationship with me, but he enjoyed my company and friendship. I was not ready for a serious relationship, but because of everything I had just been through my broken heart was wide open and vulnerable. James was not wise enough to see the dangers of our situation and I was not strong enough to let go of his friendship until the heart damage was already done.

The Word tells us that all things work together for the good of those who love God, and I know that the Lord did use James for good in my life. In this relationship the Lord showed me that it was possible for me to have a pure relationship with a man. Only once did I ever give James "that look" and he called me on it immediately. We had been rollerblading by the beach, then we took a midnight swim, and went back to his apartment. Standing in his kitchen, very late at night, my flesh reared its ugly head: I felt intensely that I wanted to be with James sexually, so I looked at him in a provocative way for just a moment. Abruptly he asked, "Why are you looking at me that way?"

"I know. I need to go," I responded. I could have tried to seduce him, but I really didn't want to. I wanted to walk away and I did! Many times I had considered having self sex while thinking about him, but the Lord gave me the strength to walk away from that temptation every single time. I knew that he was not ever going to be my husband. (And let me tell you that even if you know your boyfriend is going to be your husband, you still should not have self sex thinking about him and I will explain more about that later.) And while I was tempted about being with James, I never followed up my thoughts by acting sinfully towards him. While my hurting heart longed to be loved, I knew that I wanted to be a pure woman, and the Lord gave me that victory with James. Unfortunately, I also received a very broken heart from that relationship, but the Lord carried me through it all.

I mentioned "that look" because there are so many things that our flesh has learned by living in the ways of the world, and they are not easily forgotten. Our flesh exists to sustain itself, and if you give your flesh an inch, it will take you a mile. If I had persisted beyond the sexual glance (that I never should have given) and made a real effort to seduce James that night, I hope that he would have resisted, but he may not have. My flesh was ready to go for it, but my spirit had grown strong enough to overpower my flesh. But just being in a man's apartment at 1:00 am was foolishly giving the enemy an easy opening to lead me into sin.

A lot of times, in fact, more times than not, we place ourselves in very compromising positions, and then we act surprised that we sin. We think, "How did that happen?" I can almost guarantee you that if you backtrack through the chain of events that took place just before the sin was committed, you will find the answer as to how your sin happened. If we were to be completely honest about the sin in our lives, most of the time we walk (or even jump) right into sin, rather than helplessly fall into sin, as we like to pretend.

Think about this: when we are walking, we see what is in front of us, one step at a time. We have time to make decisions. We have time to think about the next step that we are going to take. If we have fallen, it's usually because we were tripped up all of a sudden, or lost our balance, and fell flat on our faces. Or we step into a hole, are taken off guard, and we fall down. See the difference?

The difference between premeditated murder and manslaughter also demonstrates the point well. There is also premeditated sin. But we can use the wisdom of the Word of God to learn so many practical tools on how to live our daily lives, including how to avoid sin. We can set up our own roadblocks, or sin blocks as I prefer to call them, to help prevent a lot of sin from taking place in our lives. A wise person will do this. A wise person will meditate on avoiding sin and prepare herself in order to prevent sin in her life, moving with caution, and armed with spiritual weapons, in her day-to-day life.

*Therefore let him who thinks he stands take heed lest he fall. No temptation has overtaken you except such as is common to man; but God is faithful, who will not allow you to be tempted beyond what you are able, but with the temptation will also make the way of escape, that you may be able to bear it.*

*Therefore, my beloved, flee from idolatry. I speak as to wise men; judge for yourselves what I say.* 1 Corinthians 10:12-15 *(NKJV)*

That night in James' apartment, I was walking towards sin, but fortunately I was walking with enough caution to visualize the chain of events that could take place if I did not get myself out of there quickly. I was acting very foolishly and I am thankful that God gave me the wisdom to see that before I walked into sin. It's never too late to flee from sin, but it is much easier to turn and flee when the sin is still way out in front of you, in the distance. Once you are face-to-face with the sin, it is more difficult to flee from it; to resist that temptation. My sin that night was just an arm's length away--I could reach out and touch it. Though I was face to face with sin, when I realized it, I did flee, as quickly as I could. But I should never have put myself in that position to begin with.

That night at James' apartment is etched in my memory for two reasons: because of the victory over sin that was accomplished that night, and because of what happened when I got back to my place afterwards. (By this time I had moved out of the house in which Scott and I had lived; I was renting an apartment with the girls). As I was walking from my car toward my front door, suddenly and, it seemed, out of nowhere, Scott appeared. He was very angry and made hostile remarks and accusations toward me. He made some false, but not unreasonable assumptions, considering I was arriving home in the early morning hours. But the most surprising thing for me was that his words, though extremely unpleasant, were not devastating me, as they had been in the past.

Scott's words did cause me to feel pain in my soul, but for a different reason than they had before. As he was voicing all kinds of evil about me, I looked at him for the very first time with the eyes of Christ and realized just how very lost he was. I felt compassion for him because of his sin and because of the darkness that filled his life. Knowing the truth of my identity in Christ, I could listen peacefully to what he was saying without even feeling the need to defend myself, even though what he believed about me and what he was saying about me were lies. I knew that I had just experienced a great victory in my life and that I was not the person Scott was talking about anymore--not the immoral woman who Scott had helped create. I was a new creation in Christ and it did not matter what words mere man said to me. The only words that mattered in my life were the words that Christ spoke to me. The Lord gave me great strength in the parking lot that night; I felt the power and presence of God in an almost tangible way. My sins had been forgiven and I knew it, so although the names that Scott was calling me might have been true of me at one time, they no longer rang true in my present, or for my future.

Though God and I stayed very close during this time in my life, the enemy had not given up trying to lure me back to my old ways. Not long after I was baptized, in the fall of 1995, I was working as a personal trainer in a well-established gym catering to a wealthy, sophisticated clientele. Upon overhearing me tell another trainer that I did not have enough money to get a divorce, one of the gym members introduced himself to me as an attorney and offered to help. He suggested that I meet with him at his office because he would be willing to represent me for a very reasonable fee. I met with him several times, discussing the issues of the case including custody and child support.

My meetings with the lawyer were always strictly business, except for the time I talked to him a bit about how important to me my relationship with Jesus was. I had never given any thought to this man in a sexual way and had never done anything to give him the idea that I was attracted to him physically. What I did not know at the time was that this lawyer also had been in contact with Scott, who had told him about some of my sexual activities of the past, including my attempt to seduce the neighbor. I suppose because of the things Scott told him, he devised a plan and one Friday afternoon he called and asked me to meet him at his office on Saturday morning to discuss some pressing issues related to my case.

When I arrived at his office on Saturday, he explained that I had not paid him any money yet towards my divorce, and because of that, he was not officially my lawyer *at the present time*. He explained to me that if I could come up with the money within a month, his law firm would still take my case, but that another lawyer in his firm would represent me. He reiterated this statement several times, that even if I paid his law firm, *he* personally would not be my lawyer. He even asked that I restate to him what he was telling me, "So that I can be sure you understand, that *I* am not your lawyer, and *you* are not my client." Still unsure about the purpose of this conversation, I assured him that I understood and

I did repeat this understanding back to him. As soon as I finished speaking, the lawyer rushed from behind his desk, threw his arms around me and tried to kiss me! Speechless and in shock, I pushed him away. But my mind was racing; in my mind I cried out to God, "I can't believe this is happening! I have done nothing to entice this man! Why is this happening to me? In no way, form, or fashion, have I led this man on. Why Lord? Why, Lord, are men treating me this way?"

Though I refused to let him kiss me, he didn't give up. Flabbergasted, I listened as he proposed an arrangement whereby he would set me up in an apartment, pay for all of my expenses, and give me a car. Indeed, he would take very good care of me financially, he promised. But my amazing God showed up for me! He gave me the strength and courage to decline all that the attorney suggested, and He empowered me to graciously tell him that my life now belonged to Jesus Christ, and that I was no longer that woman who my husband had told him about.

Naturally it bothered me immensely that when this man found out about my past he assumed that he could treat me as a sex object. I believe that God wants all of us to treat each other respectfully, no matter what kind of past we may have had, and without regard even to what someone's current living situation might be. Sin is sin, and God hates it; but a person is a person, and He loves all of us. Please always remember that. What this man did to me was very demeaning, but instead of becoming enraged, God gave me the mercy to recognize that he was just lost and he needed a Savior too. Jesus died for the whole world, including him.

I am so thankful that I was full of the strength of the Lord while in the lawyer's office, but when I walked out the door, I became very distraught. The enemy was bombarding me with thoughts and accusations. I was near Mark's house and I confess that I came very close to calling him. The ideas running through my mind included things like, "I have not had sex with anyone in six months and I thought I was really changing. But maybe I haven't really changed at all. Maybe I can never stop being this immoral, sex-obsessed woman. Maybe men will never look at me any other way. Maybe I will never find a man who wants the *heart* of Stacey, instead of the *body* of Stacey. Maybe I need to just give up. Maybe I should just call Mark. Maybe I should...." And then the Holy Spirit flooded my thoughts, reminding me of this verse –

*No temptation has overtaken you except such as is common to man; but God is faithful, who will not allow you to be tempted beyond what you are able, but with the temptation will also make the way of escape, that you may be able to bear it.* 1 Corinthians 10:13 *(NKJV)*

When I remembered that verse, instead of calling Mark, I called James. He was home and I drove over to his place immediately, where he, his housemate and I enjoyed a beautiful sunny day in South Florida. We laid blankets out on the grass and read The Word. The guys prayed with me and encouraged me in the Lord. I *was* a new creation in Christ. The attorney was wrong about me. The enemy was wrong, and, with great enthusiasm, I screamed out to Satan, "You are wrong about me! I am covered in the Blood of Jesus Christ! Now flee, you pathetic little thing!"

I had been very passionate while living in my sin, and I was still a person of great passion; but now I was learning how to allow Christ to be the master of my passion. I demonstrated that in the lawyer's office by my actions. I didn't just turn down his proposal (which in a sense would have made him my master); I followed up by telling this man about Jesus, my Master and Savior! You see, my friend, I was learning that Jesus is my defense, my only defense, and the only defense I will ever need. I need no other words to say, other than Jesus Christ, and Him crucified. In the final analysis, that is all I know to say to people about my past, about my present, and about my future. This life is all about Jesus, His death, and His resurrection!

*For I determined not to know anything among you except Jesus Christ and Him crucified.* 1 Corinthians 2:2 *(NKJV)*

I can imagine that you are thinking, "Seriously Stacey? On top of all those wild escapades, an attorney wanted to make you his 'kept woman'? Did all of these things *really* happen in your life?" Yes, all of these things did happen to me. I was growing in the Lord, and the enemy did not like it one bit. He used a host of wicked schemes and evil tactics to attempt to lure me back into the ways of the world. I can only imagine that I was scaring the enemy frightfully by being on fire for Jesus Christ! I pray that you, my reader, will also frighten the enemy mightily by the way you lead your life. He may come against you, time and time again, but stand strong! You can do all things through Christ who strengthens you. If you are being tempted by something, or someone, know that the

Lord always provides a way of escape. You must look for it and take it, so that you will bear the temptation with victory. Though you experience the temptation, resist and flee. Do not ever lose heart. Do not ever give up. Work out your own salvation with fear and trembling.

*Therefore, my beloved, as you have always obeyed, not as in my presence only, but now much more in my absence, work out your own salvation with fear and trembling; for it is God who works in you both to will and to do for His good pleasure.* Philippians 2:12-13 *(NKJV)*

God will work in you both to will and to do for His good pleasure. He wants to blow your mind. Since I gave my life back to the Lord, He continually blows my mind! He is such an exciting God!

## Against My Will

Months passed and I was continuing to grow in the Lord, but I still struggled with self sex on a regular basis. I felt that since I wasn't married, it was better to have self sex than to be fornicating. By this time I had thrown away all of my sexual devices and I had not watched pornography since Scott had moved out. Though I was learning how to control the thoughts in my mind concerning sex, I wasn't yet walking in complete victory in this regard.

By December of 1995 it had been nine months since I had had sex with anyone. For a woman who had had immoral sex nearly every day for years, that was a huge accomplishment. After church one Sunday I spoke to my pastor, sharing that though I was rapidly growing in the Lord, I could still sense my fleshly desires inside of me. I told him that I was keeping a handle on my flesh but I knew that it was by no means completely dead yet, and I had the uneasy feeling that I might still mess up badly. Though I didn't understand it at the time, the Holy Spirit was giving me the spiritual wisdom to appreciate my vulnerability and to watch out for the dangers of my flesh.

Pastor Bob recommended that I attend a class called Crossroads that was offered at our church one night a week. Crossroads was an addiction ministry designed for people who were controlled by a stronghold sin. I had just learned about stronghold sin through the teachings of my pastor. A stronghold sin is a sin that you really want to stop committing, but despite great personal effort, you keep committing that sin. I recognized that sexual sin was a stronghold sin for me. I truly wanted to stop committing sexual sins, such as self-sex, and to be completely pure; and I wanted to stop even desiring sex, until it was God's time for me to get married again. I wanted to rid my mind of all of those horrible pornographic images. Though I truly wanted to be set free, I had not been able to escape being bombarded by thoughts of sex. I was not holding onto sexual sin; I had let go of it, but sexual sin was holding onto me. That is, sexual sin had a "strong hold" on me.

*For though we walk in the flesh, we do not war according to the flesh. For the weapons of our warfare are not carnal but mighty in God for pulling down strongholds* 2 Corinthians 10:3-4 *(NKJV)*

Pastor Bob knew that Crossroads would teach me the weapons to use for this spiritual warfare going on in my life. He urged me to attend when the new session of Crossroads started after Christmas. I felt encouraged by what Pastor Bob told me about the class and I was very excited to be able to begin the class. Even though I was not sure how I would find a babysitter for my four little girls (because this class was taught in the evenings and no childcare was provided), I knew God would make a way because this class was exactly what I needed.

There was a very good reason that I was feeling uneasy about the possibility that I could or would mess up badly. I had been talking to a man named Clint on the phone for several weeks and my flesh was being aroused. The company I worked for wanted to advertise in the local Christian directory so I contacted the directory and started discussing with Clint the details of placing our advertisement. During a series of phone calls, Clint and I discussed all of the options, and we began to talk about things other than just business. He was a Christian man who had a very nice voice. I was not looking for this temptation to cross my path, but here I was again, faced with sexual temptation. Because my flesh was still warring against my spirit, I found myself attracted to a man I had not even met face to face yet!

We talked for hours one evening on the phone, and he told me he had been addicted to crack for years but now was walking strong with the Lord, drug-free for almost a year. The alarms should have been going off in my mind, saying, "WARNING! Wake up and listen, Stacey!"

But I really was still quite naïve, not realizing it would be a dangerous thing to put two former addicts together, especially two who had been experiencing victory for less than a year. After he told me his story, I did the worst thing that I could possibly have done: I shared *my* story with him. Why, oh why, didn't I take the advice that Brad had given me about that months earlier?

What I learned the hard way I must share with you ladies, praying you will not make the mistakes I made: *Do not* communicate about your sexual past to any man until you know the Lord is calling you to be his wife. When we share about our sexual past with a man, we are placing right in front of him temptation that he should not have to face. You should not be telling every boyfriend in your life the things that you have done sexually. I realize that by publishing this book I am sharing my sexual past with everyone who reads it, but I believe this is an appropriate exception because I *know* the Lord called me to write this book, for the purpose of leading women across the world out of bondage and into victory over sexual sin. If my book ends up in the hands of a man, especially a man who knows me well, then I earnestly pray that he will look at me through the eyes of Christ. The Lord is longing to set women free through my testimony, so I cannot suppress my story because a man might read it and become aroused. I was wrapped in very heavy chains, a slave to the demonic world. *No one* should find anything exciting about that. In fact, I would warn that anyone who finds my testimony enticing must be, as I was, entrenched in evil. That person must start praying immediately to be set free from sexual bondage!

For Christmas that year the girls and I were going to spend two weeks visiting family in Texas. Clint urged me to meet him before I left. He was preparing to leave town also, so we agreed he would come to my apartment at 6:00 am, the only time we were both available. You can probably guess that this was one of the biggest mistakes I've made in my life. Sometimes I had wisdom, but at other times, I was as foolish as they come! My girls were all sleeping in their rooms and Clint and I went into my bedroom to talk. Even though I understand (now) that going to the bedroom could easily give an unintended message to Clint about my intentions, I really believed and intended that all we would do there was talk. I had already spoken on the phone with him about how I loved the Lord and that I had been walking closely with Him. I had thirty-three Jesus posters hanging on the walls of my bedroom wall and I was filled with the desire to be a pure woman.

We did talk, but then he began to kiss me. I told him no, not to kiss me, but he continued. I begged him to stop, but it became clear he had no intention of stopping. Though I didn't try to hit or hurt him, I did try to physically push him away. I didn't scream because my young girls were sleeping in the other room. I didn't know what to do; I just knew that I kept saying no and he was not listening to me. Sexual intercourse began to take place, despite the fact I was begging him to stop--quietly, of course, so as not to wake my girls.

When he was done I asked him to leave my apartment immediately, before my daughters woke up for school. I cried and cried. Though I truly had not wanted this to happen, I felt that it was, nonetheless, my fault. "Look, Stacey," I scolded myself, "You let a man into your bedroom and got what you deserved." As I showered, I kept telling myself that it was all my fault, that I *was* an "f-ing whore," as I had been told so many times before. That particular phrase kept ringing in my mind. With what had just taken place, the enemy was taking the opportunity to tell me that it didn't matter how many Jesus posters were hanging on my walls, that is who I would always be, and that going to church would never change who I really was.

Months later I realized that actually I was raped that morning. When a woman begs a man to stop, and that man proceeds to have sex with her, she is being raped. No matter what the scenario, if she is saying NO, the man who doesn't respect that is raping her. At the time it happened, because of my past, and because of the enemy's accusations, I just didn't see it that way. Instead, I felt that I had gotten what I had deserved. I had been treated as worthless for so long by my husband that it wasn't at all strange to me to be treated as worthless by another man.

This incident caused me to mourn for weeks. I considered that my whole nine months of victory had been thrown out the window. The girls and I did go to Texas for the Christmas holidays, and I knew that I was supposed to go back to Florida because God had already made that clear to me. Remember that God-story with my keys being lost? That had taken place months earlier, so I knew that I had to return, I just wasn't sure why. Even though I didn't understand what He was doing, I knew I had to be obedient to the Lord; and I reminded myself of how excited I had been to begin my church's spiritual warfare class called Crossroads. If nothing else, this incident reinforced to me how weak and damaged I still was.

Back in Florida, and having made babysitting arrangements, I arrived at church for the first session of Crossroads only to find that Clint was there too. Within 24 hours of leaving my apartment that morning, he had gone out and used crack again, initiating a drug binge of several weeks. Finally, he admitted himself to our church's half-way house drug rehab program. Attending the Crossroads class was one of the house requirements. So, there we were, face to face, attending the same addictions class together.

I was feeling very reluctant to share these next events with you and as I sat on my front porch drinking my morning coffee, watching the fall leaves blowing off of the trees, I asked the Lord, "Do I really have to tell them? It's so embarrassing, so humiliating and just so messed up." I already knew the answer, before I even asked my Father that question. He will not let me escape sharing the details of my testimony with the world. He wants everyone to know the effects of sexual sin. He wants the world to know the tricks your mind will play on you, and the traps the enemy will set for you. He wants the world to know all the pain that ensued from playing those simple little games of lust and fantasies.

So what is it that I don't want to tell you? I had sex with Clint again. Why would I do that? Why would I be with a man again who took advantage of me? Well, at the time, I did not see it that way. I was still blaming myself for what had happened, because I thought so poorly of myself. I was just that "kind of a girl." But since it had been such a bad experience for me, I guess in a very twisted way, I wanted to have sex with him one more time to somehow make that bad memory go away. I think somehow I thought that if I willingly had sex with him, then I wouldn't feel so bad about the first time. I know—it was bizarre, messed up thinking. But distorted minds think messed up things. My mind was not listening to God's direction, and I couldn't even reason logically. Even worse, I actually believed what I was thinking was true, which is to say I didn't realize my thinking was messed up.

Maybe there is a woman reading this book right now who has had sex with a man even though she really didn't want to have sex with him. Perhaps you told him "No," but he continued to force himself upon you. Maybe you felt like it was your fault, and maybe you are still with this man who actually raped you at one time. Please realize that *I should never have allowed this man to touch me again. I should have called the police that very morning and told them that I was raped.* Let those be the words that guide the decisions that you make. But if an event like this happened in your past, let me assure you that now, over seventeen years later, I do not even remember this man's last name. I have forgiven him and, I am thankful, the Lord has completely healed me from the pain that was inflicted upon me that day.

## Keys to Victory

"You love your sin more than you love your God," the Crossroads pastor announced at the outset. Well that got my attention, and it made me mad. How dare he say that! I loved the Lord with all of my heart. I had been fighting with everything inside of me to walk with Him. How could he say that to me? I did *not* love my sin more than I loved my God! That's what I thought then, but I came to understand and agree that this teaching was true. It took me some time to see it, but, through Crossroads, I learned that I did love my sin more than I loved my God. It took time to gain wisdom, knowledge, and understanding of the things that had taken place in my life spiritually. Crossroads gave me the keys to victory, and I am going to share them with you.

To begin with, all of us in Crossroads thought that we had a major problem in our lives, whether it was sex, drugs, alcohol, anger, or unforgiveness. Whatever our experience, we were all there thinking, "I have a major problem in my life." My thought was that I was addicted to sex, and that this was the huge problem in my life. I focused on this problem every day of my life; it consumed my life, my thoughts, and my actions. "This problem" got almost all of my attention. You may be thinking, "And so it should have been Stacey. That was a big problem and you needed to be focused on it, and trying to solve that problem."

But Crossroads taught me a whole new way of thinking. You see, my friend, my thinking was all wrong, and *thinking wrongly* was the basis of the real problem! The enemy had me exactly where he wanted me. The enemy told me the lie that I had a problem with sex, because the enemy wanted me to keep my attention exclusively on sex. Let me explain.

Our Crossroads pastor taught us that rather than having problems with alcohol, drugs, sex, food, anger issues, or the like, our problem was that we focused our thoughts on our so-called "problem" instead of focusing our attention on the Lord. "The enemy has made you take your eyes off of the Lord, and he is having you focus on this make-believe problem. Focus all of your attention on the Lord, stop thinking about your problem, and the problem you think you have will then disappear right before your eyes. When your eyes are focused solely on the Lord, on His Goodness, His Righteousness, His Majesty, His Redeeming Power, His Deliverance, His Authority, His Love, your life will be completely changed."

There were no twelve steps at Crossroads. There was only one step, and that step was for one's life to be completely consumed with worshipping the Lord. Worship Him and get into His Word! Worship Him and get into His Word! That was preached over and over again. Our leaders urged us to memorize The Word, and not just a few verses. At Crossroads we were encouraged to memorize a whole chapter out of the Bible, and to choose a chapter that meant a lot to us personally. I loved Romans 8 and that was the first chapter that I memorized. By the time I finished memorizing that whole chapter, I was set free from my stronghold sin. When you memorize The Word, you are necessarily meditating on it day and night, becasue that is, after all, the only way to memorize. You have to repeat the words over and over again in your mind in order to memorize. I had written copies of the verses posted all over my desk area at work. I had to look at them again and again, in order to memorize all of them. Romans 8 is not a short chapter and though it took me a while, it was well worth the effort, since that chapter forever changed my life!

I so very much desired to be set free from sin, and that intense, sincere desire is an essential key to overcoming a stronghold sin. I began to hate my sin; it began to literally sicken me. I no longer looked upon it with a longing, wishing that I could do it, but knowing that I shouldn't do it. Honestly, for a long time I had looked at my sin as something I enjoyed doing but that I knew I shouldn't do it. It wasn't until my sin sickened me, until I saw my sin for what it really was, that I was set free. And the way that my sin began to sicken me was by my worshipping my Lord all of the time. When I took my eyes off of my sin, placed them completely on Jesus Christ, through worshipping Him and memorizing His Word, then and only then, did I see my sin for what it was.

Sin is from the pit of hell. Sin is evil. Sin is gross. Sin is demonic. Sin kills. Sin destroys. Sin is ugly. Sin is nauseating. Sin steals my life from me. Sin steals my heart from me. Sin steals my joy. Sin steals fulfillment in my life. Sin brings sorrow. Sin brings destruction. Sin shatters all that is good. Get the picture? I could keep going.

Our flesh glamorizes sin, but The Holy Spirit will truly show you what sin looks like. Do you want to know what your sin really looks like? Do you want to see your sin for what it really is? Do you want to see with your eyes your very own personal sins that you have committed? I will share with you a revelation that the Lord gave me years ago about my own personal sins.

I love illustrations. I use them to visualize things that help me learn and understand concepts, and the Lord knows that about me. This illustration will work if you have seen the film *The Passion of The Christ*. The crucifixion that takes place in that movie is incredible, even though it still is considerably less horrible than the actual crucifixion of our Lord Jesus Christ. The Word tells us that He was marred beyond human recognition. That means that if you were looking at the Cross you would not have been able to be sure that it was a human being hanging on the Cross. Understand? He was so badly beaten that He did not even look like a human.

*Just as there were many who were appalled at him, his appearance was so disfigured beyond that of any man and his form marred beyond human likeness.* Isaiah 52:14 *(NIV)*

I went with a group from our church to watch *The Passion of The Christ*. Laying in my bed after waking the next morning I was considering the crucifixion and how horrific that part of the movie was. I kept replaying images of the flogging and the crucifixion itself in my mind. While I was thinking about these things, the still, small voice of the Lord spoke to me. He said, "That is what your sin looks like. That is your sin on Me." I have always known that our sins put Jesus on the Cross, including my sins specifically, but I had never visualized it in the way that the Lord defined it to me on that morning.

He showed me that the arousal that sexual sin gave to me, as a human, were the deep cuts made by the crown of thorns. The excitement that sexual sin gave me were the holes made by the nails that pierced my precious Savior's hands. The feelings in my human flesh of sinful sexual gratification were the feelings that my Redeemer had to experience while being flogged with pieces of charred glass. As I was breathing life into my sexual sin by watching pornography, my gracious God was gasping for breath, hanging on the Cross, suffocating and dying. He had to suffocate and die because He knew that my sin was going to suffocate me and kill me. He had to die, in order for me to live. He had to die, because He knew that I was not going to let go of my sin, unless He bore *my* personal sin, unless He took *my* sin upon Himself, and unless He then could show me The Way to everlasting life. Sin is not pretty. Sin is death by crucifixion, but not *my* crucifixion. My sin and your sin, my friend, was Christ's crucifixion. He who knew no sin became sin for us.

*For He made Him who knew no sin to be sin for us, that we might become the righteousness of God in Him.* 2 Corinthians 5:21 *(NKJV)*

Whatever your sin is right now in your life, look at it with those eyes. Watch *The Passion of The Christ* and know that every stroke of the human hand that tortured our Lord's body was our sin, is our sin. But the Lord wants you to make it even more personal. As you watch Him take every affliction upon His Body, know, see, and realize that is *your* sin. That is what your sin did to your Savior. That is what your sin really looks like right now, at this very moment. See your sin for what it's worth. Stop glamorizing sin. See where your sin leads, and then see His Blood dripping down from the Cross. The afflictions placed upon our Lord's body are all of our sins, but the blood that He shed for us flowed out from those afflictions. His blood covered the sins of the world. Our sins created His wounds. He endured the wounds, which led to his death; and His death, provided for our redemption.

*Surely He has borne our griefs and carried our sorrows; yet we esteemed Him stricken, smitten by God, and afflicted. But He was wounded for our transgressions, he was bruised for our iniquities; the chastisement for our peace*

107

*was upon Him, and by His stripes we are healed. All we like sheep have gone astray; we have turned, every one, to his own way; and the LORD has laid on Him the iniquity of us all. He was oppressed and He was afflicted, yet He opened not His mouth; he was led as a lamb to the slaughter, and as a sheep before its shearers is silent, so He opened not His mouth.* Isaiah 53:4-7 *(NKJV)*

After I memorized Romans 8, while attending Crossroads, I was hooked! I became a memorizing junky. I knew that there was power in The Word and I could not get enough of it. I am the sort who goes to extremes--that's just the way I tick. I never do anything half-heartedly. Within months, I had five full chapters of the Bible memorized and it took me 25 minutes to repeat them. Walking along the beach one day I told one of my closest friends that The Word was the T-bone steak in my life. She wanted me to recite for her all of the chapters that I had memorized, and she was amazed that for 25 minutes I had The Word spilling out of my mind, my heart, and my soul.

I did not flaunt my memorization to my friends, and I never memorized for prideful reasons. Instead, I memorized because I wanted to have all of that power in me at all times. I was falling so deeply in love with Jesus that I wanted to know His Word. It seemed that memorizing and meditating on His Word was the only thing that could quench this deep desire for Him inside of me. His Word is alive and active. His Word made me feel alive, and it was actively changing my life day by day.

## New Vision

Several tremendous things took place while I attended Crossroads. The Lord gave me my very first vision, and on the day of that vision, I was set free from my stronghold sin of having self sex. In order not to ever forget it, a few days after it happened, I wrote down a full description of the vision and the explanation that the Lord gave me. The vision, truly a gift to me from the Lord, took place in February of 1996; I wrote about it in the third person, and called it *Divine Deliverance.*

# DIVINE DELIVERANCE

*It was a beautiful Saturday morning. The sun was shining ever so brightly and the birds were singing in the background. She knew that this was the day that the Lord hath made; she truly was glad and rejoicing in it. Her hands were busy cleaning, for that very night a prayer meeting was going to take place in her home. She was as high as a kite, for Jesus was the Lord of her life. The Christian music was playing vibrantly and she was singing songs to her precious Savior.*

*Then, once again, it started happening. It had been awhile but she knew what was going to take place. You could see the pain written all across her face. The shades were drawn closed and the music was turned off. She did not want to go down this path because she loved Jesus and she knew how evil it was, but yet she still committed her sin. The light and the radiance which abounded a few minutes earlier turned into darkness, and there was now emptiness within her home, and within her heart. Her soul became numb because she knew that she had just satisfied Satan and saddened her sweet Savior.*

*She began to weep and cry out to Jesus saying, "How can this still be happening? After all of these months, why won't this sin go away? I pray all of the time, go to church, go to Crossroads, listen to Christian music, and fellowship with other Christians all of the time. I'm doing everything I possibly can. I have 30 Jesus posters on my bedroom wall. I'm such a joke, Lord. I'm doing something wrong."*

*As the tears flowed down her face, she was seeking the Lord with all of her heart. She was totally beaten up and bruised from sin, and Christ had mercy and compassion on her. He told her to cleanse her mind. Over and over again He said, "Cleanse your mind. Cleanse your mind." She sat there in her chair, with her eyes closed and her hands folded. Somehow the Lord completely emptied her mind from all thoughts. After about five minutes of meditating on cleansing her mind, the Lord showed up in a very mighty way. He blessed her with a vision which would be her strength for this stronghold sin that was in her life.*

*Her eyes were closed and it was as if a movie started playing as she sat back and watched. Two hands were cupped together holding a dull light, rounded object. His hands would raise slightly, close together, and then cover the object. Three or four times this scene repeated itself. Then a single flower appeared. It was a bud which bloomed magnificently. This also repeated itself three or four times. In the darkness, an angel appeared in the upper right corner, and then it disappeared. But it was as if it was still flying around because the darkness flickered with light. After several seconds of this, the next scene started. She saw pages of a book falling, as if being thumbed through. What really caught her attention was that the pages were falling to the left, instead of to the right. The Lord made this very vivid to her. And then the only way to describe the next scene is to say that she saw PEACE....complete and utter Peace, in which the Lord said her names two times. Then the Vision stopped and she knew exactly what the Lord had just showed her.*

*The hands holding the object were Christ's hands holding her stronghold sin. He carries our sin, He takes it away, and covers it in His blood that He shed for us. There's nothing that we can do to make it go away. The flower blooming was her being filled with Christ, because she was a new creation in Him. The angel that she saw was a reminder that His angels were watching over her at all times. The pages of the book represent her life and that He is with her all of the days of her life, and through all of eternity. The pages falling in that particular way showed how the Lord was with her from the beginning to the end. And then seeing the PEACE was just that, the Lord is the peace that surpasses all understanding. Whenever He said her name twice, it was filled with so much love and gentle authority. Everything is going to be okay now--now that she has received Divine Deliverance.*

*Whoever is reading this may not understand how she could be so strong and confident one minute, then fall flat on her face the next minute. This is what a stronghold sin has the capability to do. The bondage becomes unbearable and the chains become so heavy. To say that you can set yourself free from a stronghold sin is a lie from the pit of hell. It is totally impossible. The only way to be set free is through Christ Jesus. This woman never truly realized that nothing good lives within her. She was not willing to admit that everything in her, and that every part of her, was so very wicked. But on this day, she knew that she had no power in her to overcome. She was always helping in this fight, with Jesus, but it was not until she died within, from trying to fight this fight herself, that the Lord delivered her.*

*In whatever struggles you face, the Lord will fight for you. When you are drowning, He will rescue you. Don't fight and kick when you are drowning in sin, just grab hold of the Life Preserver, and allow Him to pull you in. Please do not try to fight sin in your life on your own, because there's no such thing as 'trying' in this area. There's either losing or winning, and we are all losers when it comes to sin. There is none righteous, no not one. Only through Christ Jesus will you ever be set free from your sin. The closer you get to God, the more you realize just how big He is, and how little you are.*

*This woman has been set free from this stronghold sin in her life. It was nothing that she said or did that made it happen. It was only through Christ Jesus our precious Lord and Savior--He gave her Divine Deliverance.*

O wretched man that I am! Who will deliver me from this body of death?

I thank God-- through Jesus Christ our Lord! *Romans 7:24-25a* (NKJV)

I wrote that over seventeen years ago and I am still free of that stronghold sin to this day. I received Divine Deliverance--sexual sin left my life and the stronghold of having self sex was taken from me. I was set free and I knew it. I no longer struggled with self sex. The Lord took it from me in an instant. He had allowed me to get to the very end of *my* rope, so that my eyes would truly be opened to the truth. Like so many others, I had the pride to believe that if I tried hard enough I could fix things, no matter what they were. It's an independent mindset that didn't acknowledge how much I need God.

It's not in my nature to "let go and let God." Typically, I want a part in making things happen. I want to do something about a problem and make everything okay. I wanted to help God get rid of my stronghold sin. But you see, my friend, that was impossible for me to do. I do not have that kind of power. It didn't matter how many verses I memorized, God had to be the one to set me free. He had to deliver me.

I wish I could tell you that since I walked through that experience, now I can always stay out of God's way and wait patiently for Him to move. But those who know me well know that I still struggle in this area. It is one of my greatest weaknesses. God is my life. I breathe Him in at all times, I exhale Him, His Spirit consumes me BUT my stinking flesh still wants to help Him out. How funny is that? Actually, it's not really funny; it's totally and completely ridiculous.

Often we *think* that we are waiting on God for certain things to happen in our lives, when the truth is that God is waiting on *us* to just let go of those things. Our God loves to be glorified; that is His nature. He is a God who is worthy of being glorified and He wants all the glory. He deserves all the glory! Until we let go and truly let God be in complete control, He will not get all the glory. I know that before He does certain things for me, God is patiently waiting for me to completely let go of a few personal things in my life.

On the occasion of this vision, God was waiting for me to stop trying so hard regarding my stronghold sin. He was waiting for me to finally realize that this was something way too powerful for me to control. I thought I could and should get myself out of it, with God's help of course. Human flesh, human willpower, cannot escape a stronghold sin. Only Christ, and He alone, can set us free! Stop trying to figure out ways to get out of your sin, and realize that only Jesus can get you out of the mess that you are in. He will give you Divine Deliverance when you truly let go, I promise you that. *He is the only Deliverer!*

## New Gifts

Two other things that happened in my life while attending Crossroads, I never expected or sought: I was baptized in the Holy Spirit and I received the gift of a spiritual language. I had never been taught about the baptism of the Holy Spirit at other churches that I had attended, but one night at Crossroads I went forward for prayer and the woman who prayed for me prayed that I would be baptized in The Holy Spirit. I did not think much about the prayer at the time, because I didn't even really know what she meant by that.

Backing up a bit, I had noticed that as I continued to fall more deeply in love with the Lord, I found that even though I had memorized a lot of scripture, my human words were just not expressing what I wanted to say to my Lord. I remember praying, "Lord, I love you so much but my words are not even coming close to how I feel about You. I wish that I could really express to You what is going on inside of me." It was several weeks after telling the Lord this that the woman prayed for me to be baptized in The Holy Spirit at Crossroads.

A few days after that prayer, as I was praying and telling the Lord how much I loved Him, I began to pray with unusual sounds. I had heard vaguely about the gift of a spiritual language but I had never heard a teaching about it so when I next saw my pastor I asked him about it. He told me which sermon tape to get and when I listened to his teaching I could not believe my ears! "Have you ever felt like your human words are just not enough to express your love to the Lord?" Pastor Bob queried. "The Lord will give some people this gift of a spiritual language to use to express their love to Him." Wow! That is exactly what had taken place in my life, though I had never heard anything about it before. It just happened in my life by His Spirit.

Crossroads also taught me how very important it is to worship my Lord. Listening to Christian music became a huge part of my life. I stopped listening to secular radio stations because so many of the songs were about love relationships and about having sex. I recognized that I certainly did not need to fill my thoughts with those words and ideas. Please don't misunderstand me; I am not saying that listening to secular music is a sin. I listen to some secular music now, but I often find it can be downright depressing. I would much rather be uplifted by listening to positive music, and I thrive on worshipping my Lord through music.

At Crossroads I also learned how very important it is to hide the Word of God in your heart. Jesus is the one who sets us free from our sins, but hiding His Word in our hearts gives us strength to avoid sin. By memorizing the Word of God I have spiritual tools at my fingertips to fight the battle of living in this fallen world. Sin is all around us and we need to put on spiritual armor every day, every night, in order to walk in victory.

*Your word I have hidden in my heart, that I might not sin against You!*
Psalms 119:11 *(NKJV)*

The curriculum for Crossroads included nine sessions and when the class came to an end I was totally changed. The woman who started Crossroads in January was, it seemed to me, nothing like the woman who finished the classes at the beginning of March. My chains were gone and I had been set free completely. It is so great to be free! It may sound crazy to you but even though it has been seventeen years since I was set free from my stronghold sin, I remember vividly what bondage feels like. Bondage scares me to death, and so it should. I could fall back into bondage, and to think otherwise, is to be exceedingly foolish.

*Stand fast therefore in the liberty by which Christ has made us free, and do not be entangled again with a yoke of bondage.* Galatians 5:1 *(NKJV)*

Yes, I could become entangled again. The Word espouses that truth so I appreciate that I have to be very careful. I must always stand fast in the liberty by which Christ Jesus has set me free. I cannot play around with sin. I learned my lesson. I have no desire to play with sin, because as I shared with you above, sin now sickens me. Do I still sin? Of course I do--just ask my husband and my daughters. Not one of us is perfect, but I am not trapped in sin. I do not head out the door intending to sin. I become annoyed too easily. I say things that I shouldn't. I have a sinful thought that I should not have, but I quickly recognize the sin and cry out to my Lord to forgive me, to cleanse me, and to keep me from committing this sin again. I repent and move on. Though my day is not planned for sin, I do still sin. There is a difference. I am no longer stuck in sin.

I know what spiritual anguish feels like. I walked through it and tasted it. (Did you realize that some people have actually *tasted* pain? When it is severe enough, pain will flow through your entire being, and actually has a taste.) I understand what it means to be trapped. I lived with the feeling of hopelessness thinking there was no way to escape from my sinful lifestyle. I have experienced first-hand the lies of the enemy and the evil strategies he uses in our lives. I also know what true healing feels like and what it means to be set free. I have the experience of what it feels like to have those heavy chains broken in the name of Jesus Christ. I know the Truth and Jesus is calling me to share it with the world.

When I finished Crossroads I was walking in the fullness of Christ as I never had before in my life. Grounded in the Word and a true worshipper, I was falling more in love with Jesus each day. I had been released from my chains and the weight of my stronghold sin had been lifted from me entirely. After Crossroads ended, I was thrilled to have the opportunity to attend a six-week training class to become a Crossroads small group leader. Eagerly I desired to take the things I had learned along with my testimony to help other women who were stuck in addictive sins. Later I also completed a twelve-week Biblical counseling course at my church, fulfilling a longing to learn more from God's Word, so that I could be used by God to help all sorts of hurting people around me. God had really turned my life around!

## Dating in Purity

At the time I was attending the Crossroads leader training classes our church held a picnic for the singles at a county park in Ft. Lauderdale. Around five hundred people were there and it was at that event that I met Leo. I was sitting on a bench talking with a few of my close friends, including a former stripper, a former lesbian, and a woman who had been trapped in a food addition. What a crew! I am sure we were talking about the Lord, because that's what we did, almost all of the time. In The Word we see that Jesus hung out with sinners. The four of us knew sin well, but we knew freedom in Jesus Christ even better!

That day I was wearing a baseball cap inscribed with the words "Crazy For Christ." I had designed the cap for myself because I *was* crazy for Christ, and I considered this cap to be my armor. Prior to rededicating my life to the Lord I used to work out at the gym in very skimpy attire. Now that I was truly a changed person, I felt protected in the gym with my armor on--the armor of this cap, and various Christian t-shirts. Usually I took my Bible to the gym also, using it to memorize scriptures while on the treadmill. I was a new person, and everyone at my gym saw the huge change in my life. When your heart is devoted to God, the people in your life around you should see evidence of that; they should recognize your love for God by the way you act.

*Therefore take up the whole armor of God, that you may be able to withstand in the evil day, and having done all, to stand. Stand therefore, having girded your waist with truth, having put on the breastplate of righteousness, and having shod your feet with the preparation of the gospel of peace; above all, taking the shield of faith with which you will be able to quench all the fiery darts of the wicked one. And take the helmet of salvation, and the sword of the Spirit, which is the word of God."* Ephesians 6:13-17 *(NKJV)*

Sitting on the bench, wearing my "Crazy For Christ" cap, I was suddenly confronted by a man kneeling in front of me, asking "What's your name?" I had been having a great time laughing with my friends, with no thoughts of meeting a man at the picnic, yet abruptly, out of nowhere it seemed, there he was. Just saying "Stacey" would have been too boring and since I was in a joyful mood, as I usually am, I answered, "Crazy For Christ." Whoever this man was, I wanted to be sure he knew I was in love with Jesus.

What happened that moment that I first spoke with Leo is etched in my mind forever. The bright sun was shining on Leo's face and its light was being reflected in his brown eyes. "I've never seen such beautiful brown eyes in all of my life," I thought. Though it was the sun shining on his eyes that day, in a very short time, I was able to see 'The Son' was shining through this man's life.

Actually, I had first seen Leo the week before at a birthday party, but we had not spoken. Some friends invited me to go with them to a party and when I asked where it was being held they told me it was at the home of the Crossroads worship leader. Now, I should have known who the worship leader at Crossroads was since I had attended the entire course, but for the life of me I could not recall who the worship leader was. I could not picture his face, or remember his name. During Crossroads, I had been so focused on being set free from my stronghold sin, and so focused on Jesus, I honestly had no memory of who the worship leader was. How remarkable that for weeks Leo, through the leading of the Holy Spirit, had been leading me into worship so that I could be set free from my stronghold sin, and yet the Lord had kept me from noticing him, until I could get the healing I needed. And even though I had not spoken to Leo during the party, he had occasion to meet and address my daughters. They were stomping on grapes outside on his sidewalk so he had asked them to stop making a mess; then he brought them inside and played the Sesame Street song for them on his piano. (With Leo's influence and God's leading in her life, my daughter Ashly is now leading her own Christian band....you can check them out at revelymusic.com, or on Facebook...REVELY is the name of the band.)

Back at the picnic, Leo and I spoke briefly and then everyone was called to join in a time of worship. Leo sat down next to me on a blanket and we worshipped the Lord. Although Leo didn't know it, I had already been invited to another event at his house that evening; this time it was a send-off for a missionary who was headed off to Africa. After we worshipped together at the picnic, Leo invited me to his house for the gathering that evening, and we laughed when we discovered I was already planning to be there. So a few hours later, we were worshiping together again at his place.

Several days later I was thinking about Leo's parties--how they were always focused on the Lord and included heartfelt prayer and worship. My oldest daughters suffered from severe asthma and I had been considering asking close friends to get together specifically to pray for their health. It occurred to me that Leo's house would be a great place to meet, so I called him to ask if we could hold such a prayer meeting there and if he would be willing to lead worship for the event. After making arrangements for a time to pray for the girls, Leo and I talked that day for over an hour on the phone. The Lord had brought us together in His perfect timing! That day was March 26, 1996. By God's design, I believe, it was the day that would have been my 11th wedding anniversary. It may seem rather strange to you, but I find it very beautiful. When Leo and I spoke that day, I had no idea that he was going to become my husband, but the Lord knew. It was the first anniversary that I had to face alone, after my divorce, and the Lord brought me Leo.

You may be thinking, "That's way too fast to get involved with someone, after a divorce." But God doesn't have any formulas or schedules for how he works with His children; each of us is unique. God is outside of time, and He works His ways outside of time. Please do not judge others according to *your* timetable. Yes, people need to be cautious in relationships when they are healing from the loss of a spouse by death or divorce, but it's not our place to put a time frame on what the Lord might be doing in another's life. If you are concerned, pray for the individuals to allow the Lord to have His way in their relationship. The Lord knew exactly what He was doing when He brought Leo to me. I needed an extremely God-fearing man in my life at that time, and the Lord blessed me greatly by sending me Leo.

Leo was saved on Easter, or Resurrection Sunday, 1990. He was twenty-nine years old at that time and he had been a drug addict for fifteen years. On the day he was saved, Jesus immediately took away his addiction to drugs. In addition, although Leo had dated several girls during the seven years before I met him, he had remained sexually pure since the day he asked Jesus to live in his heart. Now do you understand God's timing? God knew exactly what kind of man I needed in my life. The Lord had been preparing him for me. Refraining from sex for seven years, he had developed great spiritual strength; he knew well how to resist temptation. I was growing in the Lord at that time, but I needed someone much stronger than myself concerning purity.

The first time Leo visited me in my apartment he told me, "I want to share something with you," and he began to recite to me the entire first chapter of the book of James. He did not realize that memorizing chapters of scripture was a passion of mine, too. I responded by quoting to him all of Romans 8. We were a match made in Heaven, don't you think? I was falling for him hard and fast. During all of our dating days, Leo did kiss me, but he never touched me anywhere below the neck. NEVER! He only kissed me. Time and time again he reminded me, "You are the daughter of The King. You do not belong to me, you belong to Him. I have no business touching you."

I did not want to have any regrets in my life. I was sold out for Jesus Christ, and I really knew that there was nothing impossible for God. So even though I was very much in love with Leo, in order to be obedient to the Lord and to be certain I would not have any regrets, I called up Scott and asked him to have his girlfriend move out of his apartment. I asked him to start coming to church with me and to give God a chance in our lives. Though our divorce had already been finalized, I recognized that the Lord *could* still restore our marriage, despite all that had happened. I was willing to trust my God, because all things are possible through Him.

You may be thinking I was crazy for making that phone call, but I wasn't. I was becoming a strong, godly woman and I did not want to have any doubts in the future about whether or not I had done the right thing. Though I was falling in love with Leo, the most important person in my life was Jesus Christ. I knew I had to make that phone call. Scott did not agree to do what I asked. He proposed doing things a different way, but I told him that my way, with Jesus Christ, was the only option I would consider. So I hung up the phone, and I never looked back. I did what the Lord asked me to do, and if Scott had agreed to my request, I would have had to trust the Lord in rebuilding that relationship. I believe that I have enjoyed great peace in my spirit over the years because I obeyed God in that test of faith and obedience.

After Leo and I had been dating for three weeks, the Lord gave me my second vision. In the vision, Leo lay in a hospital bed, in a room that was entirely white; walls, floor, bed, sheets—all were white. The only color in the whole vision was Leo's brown hair. He was lying in the hospital bed and was very sick. He said my name several times, and then the vision ended. Sound unusual? Surprisingly, this vision did not scare me at all, nor did it seem evil in any way. This vision was peaceful, even though it was about sickness. I thought about the vision a lot, and told one of my closest friends about it. I shared with her my understanding of the vision, which was that Leo was going to get very sick someday, though I did not know when. I didn't tell Leo about the vision. Can you imagine if I had told him, "The Lord showed me that you are going to get very sick, but that's all I know"? The Lord gave *me* the vision, and I believed it was *for me*. I knew someday that I would tell Leo, but I knew God would show me the right time.

I considered the vision a gift from the Lord. Let me explain. Because of all that I had been through in my first marriage, I believe the Lord was presenting to me what was going to happen in Leo's future, giving me the opportunity *not* to choose that path. It was as if the Lord showed me the vision to say, "Stacey, here is what's going to happen. You don't have to do this. You don't have to choose this. I am showing you what My plans are, and you can decide what you are going to do." The Lord gave me this message only three weeks after Leo and I started dating. Although I was falling in love with him, I could still have walked away at that point, without tremendous heartache. But I just knew that God had chosen Leo for me. I also assumed that Leo was probably not going to get sick for a very long time. So I kept this vision in my heart and I did not share it with Leo. But I will continue with that part of the story later.

My relationship with Leo progressed and I fell madly in love with him. He taught me so many things about the Lord. He showed me what a truly godly man was. He respected and honored me, and became my best friend in the whole world, besides Jesus, of course. He prayed with me all of the time and read The Word to me frequently. He kissed me more passionately than any man ever had, and yet he kept his hands to himself. Now that blew my mind! He had so much self-control that I was continually astonished. And through his strength, I gained strength.

*As iron sharpens iron, so a man sharpens the countenance of his friend.* Proverbs 27:17 *(NKJV)*

As for me, I never put my hands where they should not go and never asked him to do things that he should not do. I behaved as a godly woman and I never crossed the line with him. Whenever I insisted to Leo that I was only strong because of him, he always reassured me, saying, "No way, Stacey. You are a true woman of God!" Even now, he always encourages me and uplifts me in Christ; it is his habit to build me up. Of course we have our disagreements like any couple, but we forgive one another and move on. We do not let any root of bitterness take hold, and that is the key to a great marriage. Bitterness destroys marriages, because bitterness destroys the lives of those who are bitter, and usually those around them, too.

*Pursue peace with all people, and holiness, without which no one will see the Lord: looking diligently lest anyone fall short of the grace of God; lest any root of bitterness springing up cause trouble, and by this many become defiled.* Hebrews 12:14-15 *(NKJV)*

I will never forget one night while we were dating. Leo and I kissed each other goodbye on my front porch and then I walked back inside my apartment. I sat down in my recliner and began to tell my Lord how much I was hurting. Though my heart's greatest desire was to walk in complete purity (that is, not have sexual relations with Leo until we were married), I was feeling a sense of bodily pain because I wanted so much to be with Leo physically. As I was complaining to the Lord about how painful it was, the still small voice of the Lord replied, "There's always pain when something dies. Your flesh is dying." Ah-ha! His words, which are always perfect, enlightened me! As Leo and I exercised self-control over our desires, my flesh was dying a little more every day. Indeed it was painful, because I was experiencing the death of my flesh, even at that moment. But I wasn't suffering this pain alone; the Lord was there with me. He gave me the strength to bear through the pain, though dying to my flesh was never easy. Walking in purity was a very painful experience to my flesh, but through the pain, God's purpose was being fulfilled. His purpose was my purity.

*Blessed are the pure in heart, for they shall see God.* Matthew 5:8 *(NKJV)*

Do you want to know something that *is* easy? Walking in sin is the easy way out; it is the wide road. Walking in obedience to the Lord is the tough path—a path not for pansies, so to speak. Walking with the Lord is what *real* men and *real* women do.

*"Enter by the narrow gate; for wide is the gate and broad is the way that leads to destruction, and there are many who go in by it. "Because narrow is the gate and difficult is the way which leads to life, and there are few who find it."* Matthew 7:13-14 *(NKVJ)*

Dating in purity is of the utmost importance. Dating in purity proves so many things in a relationship. Leo proved to me that he would be a faithful husband, because he was faithful to his Lord. The Lord commands us to abstain from fornication, from sexual immorality.

*Therefore put to death your members which are on the earth: fornication, uncleanness, passion, evil desire, and covetousness, which is idolatry.* Colossians 3:5 *(NKJV)*

*For this is the will of God, your sanctification: that you should abstain from sexual immorality; that each of you should know how to possess his own vessel in sanctification and honor, not in passion of lust, like the Gentiles who do not know God; that no one should take advantage of and defraud his brother in this matter, because the Lord is the avenger of all such, as we also forewarned you and testified. For God did not call us to uncleanness, but in holiness.* 1Thessalonians 4:3-7 *(NKJV)*

During those dating days, Leo proved to me that he was faithful to his Lord and that he would always follow Him; also that he was able to follow God even in the face of great temptation. A temptation is not a sin and I can assure you that Leo and I were very tempted, but with God's help we resisted those temptations.

When you date in purity you must truly learn how to work through differences. So many dating couples, faced with a difficult situation in their relationship, avoid working through it and instead use sex to distract themselves and smooth things over. Sex in a dating relationship prevents the couple from real communication. The world thinks that sex in a dating relationship communicates love, but sex outside of marriage only communicates lust. Sex outside of marriage has nothing to do with true love, nothing at all. I might be making a few people upset by that statement, but it is truth; it is God's Truth.

Sex outside of marriage proves that I have no patience; that I care only about me and my physical gratification. If I am having sex with you outside of marriage I am not honoring you or being kind to you; I am bringing harm to you. I may even think evil towards you. I may not be faithful in marriage to you. I may give up on you when things go wrong or in difficult times. Sex outside of marriage is all about ME.

Waiting to have sex in the marriage bed proves that I have patience with you. It demonstrates kindness toward you and proves I care more about you than myself, that I will honor you and want no harm to come to you. If I am waiting for sex until we are married I only think good towards you. I rejoice in you. I will believe in you, hope in you and endure through difficult times for you. I will never fail you. Waiting until marriage to have sex is all about LOVE.

*Love suffers long and is kind; love does not envy; love does not parade itself, is not puffed up; does not behave rudely, does not seek its own, is not provoked, thinks no evil; does not rejoice in iniquity, but rejoices in the truth; bears all things, believes all things, hopes all things, endures all things.*

*Love never fails.* 1 Corinthians 13:4-8 *(NKJV)*

We have no right to touch our boyfriend because he does not belong to us. Countless times Leo proclaimed to me, "You are the daughter of The King, and I have no right to touch you." And I knew that I could not touch Leo, because he was the son of The King, and his body did not yet belong to me. Marriage gives us the right to one another's bodies. In dating, you have no rights to one another. In other words, *hands off until the ring is on*, and I am not talking about the engagement ring, it must be the wedding band!

*Now concerning the things of which you wrote to me: It is good for a man not to touch a woman. Nevertheless, because of sexual immorality, let each man have his own wife, and let each woman have her own husband. Let the husband render to his wife the affection due her, and likewise also the wife to her husband.* 1 Corinthians 7:1-3 *(NKJV)*

## An Invitation

Leo knew my whole testimony and he often exhorted me by saying, "I can't even imagine you that way, Stacey. That is not who you are now. You are forgiven. You are covered in the blood of Jesus Christ. You are a godly woman." Indeed, I was a new creation in Christ. The Lord had been changing me for months, from the inside out. Sin had truly destroyed me but Jesus restored me; every fiber of my being had been cleansed and renewed in Jesus name!

I beg you, my friend, if you are struggling with an addictive sin in your life right now, please do not give up. Never give up on Jesus, because He will never ever give up on you. Do not give up. Do not give up. Do not give up! I want to shout that to you a hundred times to get my point across. His promises for you are yes and amen!

*For all the promises of God in Him are Yes, and in Him Amen, to the glory of God through us.* 2 Corinthians 1:20 *(NKJV)*

The downward spiral of sin is an intensely vicious cycle. Sin can knock the breath right out of you. There were many times I could have given up. Having read of my struggles you have seen me fall flat on my face even after I turned back to the Lord. I have been sharing with you how sin grows like yeast, and it can consume your every thought if you do not flee from it. The message I am shouting to you is, "WARNING! REPENT! TURN AROUND! LOOK AT WHAT'S AHEAD – SIN WILL GROW IF YOU DO NOT GO TO JESUS!" The enemy tricks us into believing that sin is just a fun little game that we can play with for a short while. It's your life that you are playing with and your life is very, very precious. Your life is so precious that God sent His only Son to this earth so that you could receive everlasting life.

*"For God so loved the world that He gave His only begotten Son, that whoever believes in Him should not perish but have everlasting life.*

*"For God did not send His Son into the world to condemn the world, but that the world through Him might be saved. "He who believes in Him is not condemned; but he who does not believe is condemned already, because he has not believed in the name of the only begotten Son of God. "And this is the condemnation, that the light has come into the world, and men loved darkness rather than light, because their deeds were evil. "For everyone practicing evil hates the light and does not come to the light, lest his deeds should be exposed. "But he who does the truth comes to the light, that his deeds may be clearly seen, that they have been done in God." John 3:16-21 (NKJV)*

Possibly you are reading this book and have never asked Jesus Christ to be the Lord and Savior of your life. You may have never thought of yourself as "a sinner who needs a Savior." The Word of God tells us that we all have sinned and have fallen short of the glory of God.

*For all have sinned and fall short of the glory of God Romans 3:23 (NKJV)*

Before we continue with my testimony, I would like to pause in my narrative to say a prayer with you. It's not just any prayer. It's a prayer that will change your life forever, for all of eternity! It's a prayer that will change your life, from this very moment forward. Once you pray this prayer, with complete sincerity, every step that you take will be a step that you will not be taking alone. Jesus will be carrying you for the rest of your life. His arms will surround you with His love, His Word will surround you with His Truth, and His Spirit will guide you into all righteousness.

*But what does it say? "The word is near you, in your mouth and in your heart" (that is, the word of faith which we preach): that if you confess with your mouth the Lord Jesus and believe in your heart that God has raised Him from the dead, you will be saved. For with the heart one believes unto righteousness, and with the mouth confession is made unto salvation. For the Scripture says, "Whoever believes on Him will not be put to shame." Romans 10:8-11 (NKJV)*

This prayer is the prayer of salvation. This prayer, said in faith, is the most powerful prayer on the face of this earth. You have been fighting this battle all alone. You feel beaten, bruised and defeated. You feel there's no hope in this miserable life and that no one truly cares or truly understands. You feel like there's no way out. But there is a way out, and there is only ONE WAY out. The way out is Jesus, and Jesus Christ alone. He is the only way.

*Jesus said to him, "I am the way, the truth, and the life. No one comes to the Father except through Me."* John 14:6 *(NKJV)*

His Spirit is calling you to come home. His Spirit right now is surrounding you. He desires to make His presence known in your life. He has a plan and a purpose for your life, but until you ask Him to be your Savior, He will just wait patiently for you. It's up to you to ask. He has already done all of the work. He shed His blood for you. He died on the Cross for you. He rose from the dead on the third day for you, to give you everlasting life with Him.

You may be thinking, "First I need to get my life together before I ask God to forgive me of my sins and to be my Savior." But that is not how salvation works, praise God! I was utterly unable to get my life back together in my own strength. I had to have the strength of my Lord and the love of my Lord to change my broken life. He was the One who changed me. We each receive salvation by *asking* for it. We do not receive salvation by *doing* things for it. Salvation is a gift from God.

*For by grace you have been saved through faith, and that not of yourselves; it is the gift of God, not of works, lest anyone should boast. For we are His workmanship, created in Christ Jesus for good works, which God prepared beforehand that we should walk in them.* Ephesains 2:8-1 *(NKJV)*

Would you like to receive this gift? Would you like to ask Jesus Christ to be the Lord and Savior of your life? All that you have to do is ask Him into your heart, confess your sins to Him, and believe in Him. Then you, my very dear precious friend, will be saved!

This prayer is just an example of a prayer of salvation. You can make your prayer more personal. He is waiting for you. He loves you.

"Jesus Christ, I am asking You to be the Lord and Savior of my life. Forgive me of all my sins. I believe that you died on the Cross and rose again. Come live inside of my heart. I give my life to you from this day forward. I am Yours, Lord."

If you just prayed that prayer for the very first time in your life, then welcome to the Kingdom of God! You are saved. Your life is now hidden with Christ in God. You can look forward to going to heaven when you die, to spend eternity in the presence of God.

*If then you were raised with Christ, seek those things which are above, where Christ is, sitting at the right hand of God. Set your mind on things above, not on things on the earth. For you died, and your life is hidden with Christ in God.* Colossians 3:1-3 *(NKJV)*

Maybe, like me, you once walked with the Lord, but then you fell away. Maybe you are on the downward spiral of sin right now in your life, and you feel like you are drowning in your sin. In the same way that a lost person says the prayer of salvation, a backsliding Christian can say a prayer of rededication to the Lord. That is what I did, and then I began my upward climb back to the Lord, by the power of The Holy Spirit. It's not easy to reverse the downward spiral of sin, and it's truly impossible, *unless* you cry out to Jesus Christ. He and He alone will deliver you. It's time to come back to Him, to place your life back into His Hands. Rededicate your life to Him. Drop to your knees and cry out to Him. He is there waiting for you. Please don't continue to live in your sin. Please stop letting your sin beat you up and bruise you all over. I completely turned my back on the Lord for three horrible years. I am amazed that it took me so long to come back to Him, yet I rejoice that it wasn't too late for me to return to Him, and it is never too late for you either; no matter how many years it has been.

Fall more in love with Jesus TODAY!

# SIX
# A PURE LOVE

The still small voice of the Lord spoke to me on the morning of October 2, 2011, at 4:00 am, telling me to write another book—one to accompany this book. *Fulfilling Love* is all about my testimony and the things that the Lord has done in my life. In another book, Lord willing, other women will share their stories of how Jesus Christ delivered them from addictive sins.

As you have been reading this book, you may be facing issues in your life concerning sexual sins or other sins. Some of you may be wrapped in chains by an addictive sin. Or perhaps you have already overcome an addictive sin in your life and would like to share your story. Whatever the case, I would love to hear from you. In this future book, I will compile the stories that I receive concerning women's battles against sin to share with others anonymously. My plan is to publish the stories along with my Bible-based commentary to help others learn from those experiences. Be praying about what you might share with me and at the end of this book I will tell you more about how to contact me.

If you are really struggling in a particular area at this time, consider writing down on paper the battles you are facing concerning this addictive sin. Putting your thoughts on paper as a letter to God as you are going through your struggles invites God to respond to help you overcome. If you have had victory in your life over an addictive sin, write that down, too, to share what the Lord has done in your life. Lord willing, there will be another book giving all the glory to God!

# Pit Stop for Leadership

Before continuing with my story I would like to tell you more about me. I am a mother of four daughters, have been married twice (you already know that I am going to marry Leo), and I am utterly on fire for my Lord! I like to say MY Lord because that makes Him very personal to me. I pray that He is *your* Lord too, but He is also *my* Lord, and I will shout that from the mountaintops until I take my last breath! I have one granddaughter and one grandson, whom I call "my little jewels from heaven". For eleven years I was a certified National Strength and Conditioning Association Personal Trainer. I homeschooled my daughters for nine years and I was a pastor's wife for ten years. Yes, believe it or not, the woman about whom you have been reading, who was so deeply in sin and completely trapped in darkness, was placed into the ministry by the Lord. In the World's eyes it seems impossible, but to God, it is nothing. We are the apple of His eye, *no matter what sins we have committed.* He loves us and forgives us. We are precious in His sight. Do not ever let anyone tell you anything else.

*"He found him in a desert land and in the wasteland, a howling wilderness; he encircled him, He instructed him, he kept him as the apple of His eye.* Deuteronomy 32:10 *(NKVJ)*

Now I want to address women who are in leadership positions in their churches and those who counsel or mentor other women. Unfortunately, a lot of Christians judge others very harshly, and Lord, please forgive us when we do that. When sinners come into our churches and we act shocked, or find it hard to look on their sins, shame on us! Jesus came specifically for sinners, and in my observation, it often seems that the Church as a whole has forgotten that. Wake up Church! Remember from whence tho hast fallen. Remember His Love. We are to be His hands, His feet, His words, to a lost and dying world. We are to share His Truth, but unless we share it in love, the lost want nothing to do with us.

*And when the scribes and Pharisees saw Him eating with the tax collectors and sinners, they said to His disciples, "How is it that He eats and drinks with tax collectors and sinners?" When Jesus heard it, He said to them, "Those who are well have no need of a physician, but those who are sick. I did not come to call the righteous, but sinners, to repentance."* Mark 2:16-17 *(NKJV)*

Some Christians may have the opinion that this book in your hands right now should never have been written. They may agree that my sins are covered in the blood, but believe there is no need for me to share my story publicly. But I must argue that for me to testify that I have been set free from the bondage of sin, without including any of the details of my personal experience, would not provide any help to someone stuck in similar bondage right now. When you are living in such captivity, you feel desperate for any shred of hope; any signs pointing toward a possible way of escape. You feel scared to death, and you think you are all alone. You feel certain that there's no way that anyone could understand your entrapment. The chains wrapped around you are so heavy that you can barely breathe. You think that you are never going to be free from this addiction. Women in church leadership, please try to understand the power of such bondage, if you yourself have never been trapped in it.

These women cannot fight their battles alone and they don't know who can help them. They may know that Jesus can set them free, but they don't know where to begin or how to wage war against the enemy. They may consider talking to someone at church, but they fear that no one will ever understand the depth and power of their sin. Especially if they committed these sins as a Christian, they are very ashamed of the things that they have done. Since they have never heard a Christian woman confess or discuss such sins, they imagine that it's probably unacceptable for them to talk about these sins with anyone. The shame is too heavy to bear, and they don't know where to turn or what to do.

*That* is why this book is so necessary. I, Stacey Lynn, understand these women, because I was one of them. I have been sharing my downward spiral of sexual sin with you, so that you can know that I truly do understand, and so that you, women in Christian leadership, will have a more complete understanding of deep-rooted, stronghold sexual sins. Jesus Christ truly understands these issues, of course, and He is calling all of us to understand the downward spiral of sexual sin. He is calling the Church to stop avoiding any and all mention of sexual sin. Since the world is working overtime to entice women and men (even teens and often children) into the darkness of immoral sex, the Church needs to be willing to teach, and perhaps even be aggressive about teaching, Christians how to avoid and resist sexual sin. And when necessary, we need to teach people how to become free from the bondage of these sins. Jesus Christ truly forgives ALL SIN, even the most sordid and scandalous sexual sins that a person might commit.

Christian leaders, let's be His hands to these women. Open up your hearts to them, and please listen to them. They need someone to hear their struggles. They need someone to whom they can confess their sins. They are ordinary women who, while leading typical lives, have fallen into dangerous sin. They need a real Savior and you can show them The Way. Stop judging them for their sexual struggles and the perversions that have bound them. They are wrapped in heavy chains and need help in order to be set free from. Please have God's heart for them. Let them see Jesus flowing through you. Share God's Word with them, but please, *please*, make sure that you share God's Word in love.

I believe that the Lord showed us King David's fall into sexual sin with Bathsheba so that we could truly understand David's repentance. We were given the details of David's sexual sin in The Word of God, and that is what I have done with you concerning my testimony. When I say to you, "I have been set free," you now know *from what* I have truly been set free. You can appreciate the power of God in my life because of my testimony.

I have such a heart for these women who are trapped in stronghold sins. I love them, and because I love them with Christ's love, I have been willing to confess my sins to the whole world with the hope that those women will know of my journey and feel hopeful, knowing that they also can be set free. Fervently I pray that everyone reading my testimony will recognize that you can never stray so far away from Almighty God that He is unable to save you.

As well, remember that sin is sin in God's eyes; that is, all sin separates us from God, so we mustn't consider people involved in sexual sin somehow less valuable than others. Christ demonstrated to us that His Kingdom is available to all. A drug addict, a stripper, an alcoholic, an adulterer, a homosexual, a murderer, a thief—all are invited to become adopted children of The Most High God, because of The Cross of Christ. Our sins are covered by His blood. At the Cross it's level ground; we are of equal value to our Savior. He shows no favoritism, and I love that about Him.

*For God does not show favoritism.* Romans 2:11 *(NIV)*

And that is why I, who lived in such darkness, could be called by God to become a pastor's wife for ten years. Amazing as it may seem when considering my background, I am a woman of God, because He shows no favoritism and He sees me as white as snow. His Blood cleansed me! Remember that, Christian. Remember that, Church, when sinners begin to confess wretched sins. Rejoice that He is calling sinners to Himself to repent, and come home to Him. Do not turn them away or judge them. Love them with His love. Now, back to my story.

## Engaged the Lords Way

Leo and I fell in love very quickly. Well, it seemed quick to me. This poor guy had been waiting for seven years for the Lord to bring him his wife, so, it didn't seem so quick to him. Rather than ask me to marry him, Leo asked me to attend a premarital class with him. Our church strongly encouraged couples to attend this class before setting a wedding date, so that the couple could really seek the Lord on whether or not it was His will that they marry. Walking in God's will is the way to experience true satisfaction in this life; purposefully or neglectfully living outside His will leaves us feeling empty inside.

After Leo asked me to attend the premarital class with him, I prayed to the Lord, "Is this the one You have chosen for me? Should I go to this premarital class with Leo? Is this my husband? Please tell me, Lord, what Your will is. I only want to walk in the path that You planned for me. Please tell me what to do." As I was praying, in that now-familiar still, small voice, God gave me not a specific answer, but a scripture address. He had never done that before, but on this occasion He said to me, "Jeremiah 29:11." That's all He said. At the time, I had no idea what that Bible verse contained, but I had heard those words as clear as a bell. So I grabbed my Bible and found Jeremiah 29:11 as fast as I was able.

*"For I know the plans I have for you," declares the LORD, "plans to prosper you and not to harm you, plans to give you hope and a future."* Jeremiah 29:11 *(NIV)*

Astonished, I read the words again and again. I could hardly believe that my God gave me such a specific answer. He is so real and so personal! He had become my very best friend in the whole world. He understood me, when no one else did. He loved me and cared for me in ways that no human being ever could. I trusted Him with my life and I knew that He would tell me what to do. With interactions like this one, my faith was growing by leaps and bounds. Faith is the key for spiritual growth--faith in Him, faith in His Word, faith in His promises. Faith goes beyond what our eyes can see.

*Now faith is the substance of things hoped for, the evidence of things not seen.* Hebrews 11:1 *(NKJV)*

We must have faith when we are asking Him what to do, and we must believe that He will answer.

*If any of you lacks wisdom, let him ask of God, who gives to all liberally and without reproach, and it will be given to him. But let him ask in faith, with no doubting, for he who doubts is like a wave of the sea driven and tossed by the wind. For let not that man suppose that he will receive anything from the Lord; he is a double-minded man, unstable in all his ways.* James 1:5-8 *(NKJV)*

Receiving Jeremiah 29:11 as the answer to my prayer confirmed to me that I was supposed to go to the premarital class with Leo. We attended the weekly sessions for six weeks and when the class finished, my daughters and I went to Texas for a month. It was summertime, and I wanted to spend some time with my parents and siblings. But more importantly, I wanted to really seek the Lord intensely concerning marrying Leo. Leo and I agreed it was a good idea to spend a month apart to seek the Lord, to be sure we had heard clearly from Him concerning our future.

I don't know if you have ever heard the expression "pray hard" but I am a firm believer in doing just that. I believe in seeking the Lord passionately and praying intensely, which involves pressing in with great force.

*LORD, I cry out to You; make haste to me! Give ear to my voice when I cry out to You. Let my prayer be set before You as incense, the lifting up of my hands as the evening sacrifice.* Psalms 141:1-2 *(NKJV)*

While seeking the Lord, I knew that being around Leo (for instance, having him there to kiss me each evening) would distract me from being able to recognize clearly the Lord's guidance. I was still fearful that the desires of my flesh might drown out the voice of the Lord. The last thing that I wanted to do in my life was to go in the wrong direction, apart from God's plan. I had done that before, and I didn't want to ever do that again. This fear of the power of my fleshly desires was a very good thing in that it caused me to make provisions for getting alone with God, so that He could have His Way in me.

*Teach me Your way, O LORD; I will walk in Your truth; Unite my heart to fear Your name. I will praise You, O Lord my God, with all my heart, and I will glorify Your name forevermore. For great is Your mercy toward me, and You have delivered my soul from the depths of Sheol.* Psalms 86:11-13 *(NKJV)*

Leo and I reunited after a month apart and became engaged. Since we lived in Ft. Lauderdale, I imagined that Leo might make a romantic proposal on the beach, but that was not how it happened. He came to my apartment one evening after the girls were in bed. Having just showered, I had on no make-up and my hair was soaking wet. As we sat talking in the living room, suddenly Leo bent down on one knee and asked me to marry him. I said yes, of course; we both cried, and then we prayed together. It may not sound very romantic but it was perfect! Though he was working as a janitor at our church at the time, he gave me the most beautiful engagement ring that I had ever seen.

Neither Leo nor I had very much money, but we wanted to have a traditional wedding. I did not want to ask my dad to pay for our wedding because he had already paid for my first wedding. My heavenly Father, whose resources are endless, provided for us all we could have ever wanted for our wedding. Leo and I stayed completely pure during our dating days and our engagement. God showered us with gifts for our wedding and I believe He was rewarding our purity, obedience and faithfulness. Let me tell you all that the Lord provided His beloved *pure* son and daughter, Leo and Stacey.

## Wedding Gifts

I had pictured in my mind just the sort of wedding dress I wanted: an old-fashioned, Victorian-style wedding dress with a lot of lace. A friend of Leo's knew a woman who wanted to give me her old wedding dress and when I saw it, I was surprised and thrilled, because it was exactly what I had imagined, only even prettier than I had dreamed. And, because God is who He is, it fit me perfectly, without any alterations! She gave me my wedding dress for FREE!

For the wedding, Leo wanted to wear a tux. Most men rent their tuxedos but the Lord had other plans for Leo. From time to time, a tailor who attended our church donated suits to the church. In God's perfect timing, the tailor showed up one day to donate suits, including a tuxedo that fit Leo perfectly! He gave Leo this tuxedo for FREE!

Everyone knows that wedding cakes are very expensive, even if you get them from a grocery store. Have you ever imagined what a wedding cake would cost if made to order by a pastry chef who worked at an elite, four-star restaurant in Ft. Lauderdale? I don't know what it would have cost, but that pastry chef made us a gorgeous wedding cake and gave it to us as a wedding gift for FREE!

Wedding invitations can cost a pretty penny, especially if you have them created and personalized just for your event. A graphic artist friend of mine created our invitations and she gave them to us as a wedding gift for FREE!

The Lord is interested in the details of our lives, even when it comes to coffee and peanuts; nothing is too big for our God and nothing is too small for Him either. A gourmet coffee dealer provided all of the coffee for our reception and he threw in some peanuts as well. He gave us these things as a wedding gift for FREE!

Of course a bride wants to look especially beautiful on her big day. A hair stylist did the hairstyles for me and all of my daughters on the morning of my wedding; and a very good friend of mine who is skilled with cosmetics, did my make-up. These services were all given to me as wedding gifts for FREE!

You never know when you are going to need your church family. I love that about church families; they should always be there for one another. I had no family in the area, so some of the girls I met at the Crossroads class threw a bridal shower for me. And our church family put together our whole wedding reception. Friends decorated the room and provided all of the food for the reception. This was their wedding gift to us for FREE!

During the time we were engaged, Leo was employed at our church serving as a janitor and as a pastoral intern. As a wedding gift, the church leadership bought us a room at the Radisson Hotel near the beach in Boca Raton, Florida, along with our dinner on the wedding night and our breakfast the next morning. Our church gave us these gifts for FREE!

Not all that impressed yet? Wait, there's more! We still have the honeymoon to discuss.

Another church friend of ours arranged for us to have a timeshare condominium in Hilton Head, South Carolina, for seven days! So even our Honeymoon accommodations were given to us as a wedding gift for FREE!

*Every good gift and every perfect gift is from above, and comes down from the Father of lights, with whom there is no variation or shadow of turning.* James 1:17 *(NKJV)*

To summarize, God, through His children, provided these gifts for my wedding: my wedding dress, Leo's tuxedo; our wedding cake; wedding invitations; reception fare and decorations, hair & make-up services, and accommodations for the wedding night (with meals) and for a one-week resort honeymoon! My Father in heaven totally and completely paid for my wedding—that is, *His daughter's* wedding. He paid for everything! He did far more than I could ever have asked for or imagined.

*Now to Him who is able to do exceedingly abundantly above all that we ask or think, according to the power that works in us, to Him be glory in the church by Christ Jesus to all generations, forever and ever. Amen.* Ephesians 3:20-21 *(NKJV)*

I was a pure and holy bride that day. My groom on earth saw me as pure and my groom in heaven saw me as pure. I was a virgin in the eyes of Christ. I realize that may be something that you just can't quite grasp, after everything that I have shared with you, but it's the truth; it's God's Truth! That is the only truth that matters, and that is the only truth of importance in my life. I walked in that truth on that day, and I still walk in that truth to this very day.

My wedding was absolutely beautiful. As I walked down the aisle, and as I said my vows to Leo, I was thinking about the vision the Lord had given me early in our relationship—the vision that Leo would one day become very sick. As I said my vows to Leo, and to my Lord, in the presence of the church, I was very certain that Leo was going to be ill someday, but this didn't cause me to feel any hesitation or concern. I just realized that it would be something that we were going to have to face one day in our marriage. Of course I had no idea what God had planned, and in my mind, I supposed the "sickness" part was probably ten or twenty years in the future.

Leo and I had a beautiful wedding night. We prayed before we made love and asked the Lord to bless our physical relationship. The Lord created sex, so why shouldn't we ask Him to bless our sex in the marriage bed? The Lord was with us and the Lord blessed us for maintaining purity during our dating days. No, I am not going to give you any *details* in this area, but I will encourage you that the Lord has complete control of your body when you truly hand it over to Him. The Lord can make things happen in your body when you make love to your husband. I believe that with all my heart, because I have experienced it. Before and during my engagement to Leo I walked in purity for the first time in my grown up life and my physical relationship with Leo was blessed immensely because we walked in obedience. My marriage bed with Leo seemed "out of this world," but this time it was not the dark world where I had been in the past. It wasn't the demonic world that was enticing my flesh and making my body experience sensual, exciting new things. Indeed, making love with my second husband ushered us into the heavenly realm in a way that I could never have imagined.

# A Bump in the Road

The enemy, also known as the father of lies, is a counterfeiter. Immoral, perverted sex is a counterfeit for married, godly sex. The enemy wants to deceive us into thinking that walking in holiness is boring--that walking with God is just following a bunch of rules. But those are lies from the pit of hell! The enemy is in the business of playing tricks on you. Why do people drink? They like the way it makes them feel and it can also be a way of escape from dealing with the pain that is in their lives. Why do people do drugs? They like the way it makes them feel and it is a way of escape from dealing with the pain that is in their lives. Why do people watch pornography? They like the way it makes them feel and it is a way of escape. Why do people have self sex with deceptive devices? They like the way it makes them feel and it is a way of escape. Why do people cheat on their spouses? They like the way it makes them feel and it is a way of escape. I could go on and on.

It is as simple as this: Why do we sin? We like the way it makes our flesh feel. No matter what the sin, we who are sinning are acting out in our flesh. If you become angry with someone and lash out at them with cruel words, you are doing that because it feels good to your flesh; but it's not how Jesus would have you behave. All of the sins that we commit, we commit because it feels good to our flesh. Each time we sin, we are feeding our flesh, causing our flesh to become hungrier for more. You do realize, don't you, the more that you eat, the more that you want to eat? Our stomachs stretch when we overfill them, and our stomachs can also shrink so that we do not need to eat as much and do not feel as hungry. The same thing is true of our flesh. The more you feed your flesh, the more it wants to be fed. That is how the downward spiral of sin begins. Yet the scheming enemy will seek to deceive you, asking, "How can something be so wrong when it feels so good?" Listen to me my friend, that's a trick and a lie! Remember this verse:

*...who exchanged the truth of God for the lie, and worshiped and served the creature rather than the Creator, who is blessed forever. Amen.* Romans 1:25 *(NKJV)*

That is exactly what I did in my life. I exchanged the truth of God for the lie. I fed my flesh and it felt good. And when my flesh cried out for more, I continued to feed it. In that way I began to serve the creature instead of the Creator. I loved my sin, I loved my flesh, more than I loved my God. And before I knew it, I was wrapped in heavy chains. My flesh had completely taken over my spirit.

As I said, my marriage bed with Leo was pure, but after about only a week of marriage something began to happen that shocked me. I am only sharing this with you because I believe it is very important for others to be aware that this could happen to them as well. At this point in my walk with the Lord, my spirit was much stronger than my flesh. Spiritually, I had stomped down my flesh to the bottom of my heel, so to speak. I had learned how to control my flesh and my spirit had truly taken precedence many months before. Even though I had stopped feeding my flesh, I had not completely extinguished its ability to influence my life because our flesh will never completely die until we are in heaven. We live in our flesh, and there is just no way around that one. We have to deal with our flesh every single day of our life.

When I married Leo I had not had sex since the time when I was having immoral, impure sex. My flesh had been *trained* to have immoral sex, so that is what it remembered. In fact, I had spent hundreds of hours over the years training my flesh to have impure sex. I say "training" because that is what had taken place. The Merriam-Webster's 11th Collegiate Dictionary definition for TRAIN is, "1 a. to form by instruction, discipline, or drill; b. to teach so as to make fit, qualified, or proficient; 2 to make prepared (as by exercise) for a test of skill; 3 to aim at an object or objective."

When I was on my downward spiral of sexual sin, I was initially reluctant to enter into each sin. While I resisted at first, when I eventually began to do the sins, I was *training* my flesh to do these sexual sins. Impure sex was all that my flesh knew of for years and years. Here's the thing about sex: sex is very fleshly, even when you are having pure (marital) sex. When I began making love with Leo, my husband, my flesh was awakened once again. My flesh had not experienced that kind of excitement since the days when I was living under the control of sexual sin. After about a week of marital sex, my flesh wanted to go right back to what it knew--what I had trained it to do.

Specifically, what I mean is that the images of the pornography that I had placed in front of my eyes for so many years came flashing back. My mouth wanted to start using vulgar words. My mind wanted to wander off into the fantasy world. I was shocked and troubled that this was happening to me. I knew I had been set free, that I had been delivered and loosed from the chains which had once bound me. I had walked in freedom for such a long time. The Word told me, "When the Son sets you free you will be free indeed." In panic, I thought, "Isn't that true? Wasn't I truly delivered and set free?" Only later, I realized the enemy was taking this opportunity to try to trick me again!

Leo and I talked about what was happening. We prayed about it, and we made certain to pray together prior to each time we were about to make love. Leo was so strong spiritually that he was not only able to be patient with me during that time, but he was also able to help me understand what was taking place. I *was* totally and completely set free, but the enemy was right there to tell me otherwise.

We came to realize that we just had to *retrain* my mind, and my flesh, into enjoying pure sex. I *was* set free from the chains and was a pure woman of God. But since I had not aroused my flesh since the days of immorality, I had to train my flesh to respond in a much different way now. The Lord was the one in charge this time. The Word of God became even more powerful and active to me. Taking every thought captive to the obedience of Christ became even more essential in my life, especially in my marriage bed.

*For the weapons of our warfare are not carnal but mighty in God for pulling down strongholds, casting down arguments and every high thing that exalts itself against the knowledge of God, <u>bringing every thought into captivity to the obedience of Christ</u>* 2 Corinthians 10:4-5 *(NKJV)*

*"Is not My word like a fire?" says the LORD, "And like a hammer that breaks the rock in pieces?* Jeremiah 23:29 *(NKJV)*

I share this with you because this may happen to you, after being set free from sexual sin, and I do not want you to be frightened or alarmed if it does. Perhaps it will not happen to you, but if it does, you are just going to have to retrain your mind and retrain your flesh into having pure, holy sex with your husband. You have been set free. You have been delivered. Do not listen to the lies that the enemy is shooting into your mind. The Word of God is alive and active and you need to use The Word to retrain your thoughts. Ask the Lord to take over, to teach you how to have pure sex, how to make love in purity. I promise you that He is faithful, and He will lead you in retraining your flesh on how to enjoy pure, marital sex.

*Now may the God of peace Himself <u>sanctify you completely</u>; and may your whole spirit, soul, and body be preserved blameless at the coming of our Lord Jesus Christ. <u>He who calls you is faithful, who also will do it</u>.* 1Thessalonians 5:23-24 *(NKJV)*

# Not What We Expected

For the first six months of my marriage my life was incredibly wonderful, beyond my wildest imagination! I was still totally and completely on fire for my Lord, and I was crazy in love with my husband. (I am a very passionate person in all areas of my life, and always have been.) Our physical relationship was blessed beyond measure. Having been completely healed from the damage of my past, it seemed that things were about as good as they could possibly be, while still living on Earth.

But one night, Leo developed a fever with chills and woke up the next morning with pain in his lower legs. He called in sick for his job and stayed home. One day turned into two days. Two days turned into three days and his sickness did not leave him. We started seeing doctors to find out what was wrong with him. Days turned into weeks, weeks turned into months, and months have turned into years. My husband has now been sick for fourteen and a half years. I could write another book about his illness and his years of being a pastor, and the way God has faithfully walked us through all the challenges and struggles we have experienced along the way.

Through all these years, I have learned well that the Lord always has a plan and a purpose, even when we do not understand His reasons. We just have to trust Him, and continue to walk with Him by faith. He is in control. He knows what He is doing. His ways are not our ways, yet He has a perfect plan and we must trust Him.

*"For My thoughts are not your thoughts, nor are your ways My ways," says the LORD. "For as the heavens are higher than the earth, so are My ways higher than your ways, and My thoughts than your thoughts. "For as the rain comes down, and the snow from heaven, and do not return there, but water the earth, and make it bring forth and bud, that it may give seed to the sower and bread to the eater, So shall My word be that goes forth from My mouth; it shall not return to Me void, but it shall accomplish what I please, and it shall prosper in the thing for which I sent it.* Isaiah 55:8-11 *(NKJV)*

So my vision had come to pass only six months after I married Leo. At that point, everything in my life changed drastically. I was (and still am) a very healthy, very passionate woman, married to a very sick man.

The Lord has tested me greatly concerning my mind and my flesh. It has been seventeen years since I rededicated my life to the Lord. I have been married to Leo for sixteen years. He has been sick for fifteen and a half years and for the past seven years he has been very sick. Four years ago the Lord called me to a much higher place spiritually. As a married woman, logically I should be able to make love whenever I want to, but that has not been the case for me. I will not share the details of my sexual relationship with my husband, out of respect for our privacy. I trust the Lord on these events. I simply offer that because of my past, and because of my passionate spirit, this situation has been a fiery test from the Lord.

*Oh, let the wickedness of the wicked come to an end, but establish the just; for the righteous God tests the hearts and minds.* Psalms 7:9 *(NKJV)*

*The refining pot is for silver and the furnace for gold, but the LORD tests the hearts.* Proverbs 17:3 *(NKJV)*

*But as we have been approved by God to be entrusted with the gospel, even so we speak, not as pleasing men, but God who tests our hearts.* 1Thessalonians 2:4 *(NKJV)*

This book, which I know the Lord called me to write, is coming to a close. I truly believe that the Lord has entrusted me with a very particular calling. Because He has tested me so thoroughly in this area, I know that I cannot sit back quietly and enjoy the victory He gave me without sharing it with other women. He has entrusted me with the Gospel, and He has called me to share my life with women who are wrapped in chains of sexual sin, or who have wound up in bondage to any other addictive sin. I understand what it means to be in bondage, and how it feels to live life being wrapped in the chains of heavy sin. I understand sexual sin and sexual abuse, in a way that a lot of women cannot even imagine.

God has called me to share my testimony with women in church leadership so that they will understand the power that this sin can have over a woman's life. My heart cries out to the Church. "Please *listen* to these women!" Before I was a pastor's wife, I served as a leader of a women's bible study concerning addictive sins and as a Biblical counselor through my church. As a pastor's wife for ten years I taught a ladies' Bible study twice a month for eight years. Having served in those roles, I can assure you that the women the Lord is bringing into your church have all kinds of issues. I have learned that the more open and honest you are with the women who the Lord brings to you, the more open and truthful those women will be with you. Please allow them to confess their sin, which may include their sharing of the details of their sin; and please do not treat them differently after you have heard their stories.

I could not have adequately confessed my sins by just saying, "I committed sexual sins." I had to be real. I had to honestly disclose my sins—all of them. In order to be truly cleansed from my sins, I needed to be specific in the confession of those sins. The Lord knew how far I had fallen. He was nailed to the Cross for every single sin that I committed, no matter how depraved. The Lord is not ashamed of our sins; He hung on the Cross, in front of the whole world, to die for our sins, taking on himself the punishment we deserved. Since the Lord was never ashamed of us while we were in our sins why should we feel too ashamed to confess our sins? Indeed, we should *not* feel ashamed to fully confess all of our sins because His blood covers them all, and this specific confession is what is needed for true healing.

Women like to share their hearts. They feel a need to talk about the things that they have experienced and to discuss their pain with people who care about them. This is all part of the process of gaining forgiveness, cleansing and healing.

*If we confess our sins, He is faithful and just to forgive us our sins and to cleanse us from all unrighteousness.* I John 1:9 *(NKJV)*

Until I started writing this book, I had not spoken of the sexual sins I committed for years upon years. I've been living as if I never did do these things, and most of the time I don't even remember committing these sins, because they are so deeply buried under the blood of Jesus. While reading the unfinished manuscript the other night, my daughter stated she felt that she was reading about someone else's life. She cannot even imagine me in this way at all. As I have been pressing toward the goal for the prize of the upward call of God in my life, my sins are not only forgiven but they are forgotten as well. But now the Lord has asked me to share what He has done in my life, so I have had to recall these awful events. This sharing of my testimony is part of the personal, upward call of God, in my life. I can assure you that if the Lord had not called me to do this, I would not be doing it.

*Brethren, I do not count myself to have apprehended; but one thing I do, forgetting those things which are behind and reaching forward to those things which are ahead, I press toward the goal for the prize of the upward call of God in Christ Jesus.* Phil 3:13-14 *(NKJV)*

Though it has been extremely rare in the past seventeen years that I would ever mention my past sins (I only did so in counseling sessions where I felt doing so could help another woman who was in sin), the Lord has now placed in me an overwhelming passion to help other women wrapped in chains. I realized I would only be able to help them by sharing my story in detail. The Lord desires for all women to be set free, including you who are holding this book at this very moment. He yearns to release you from your chains—He is the one who holds the key to unlock them. And He knows exactly who you are, exactly what you have walked through, how you are feeling, and what you are facing. But He also knows the grand plans that He has for you. The pivotal truth is that *until you know exactly who He is, not much will change in your life.*

## Key to Freedom

Do you really know who God is? Who is He to *you* personally? Not, who is He to your parents? Not, who is He to your spouse, nor to your brother, sister, friend, coworker or even your pastor. Who is He to *you*? Until you know in your heart who He is, you will not see much change in your life. You have to know Him personally, in order for your life to change permanently!

The first step to making a change is having the desire to change. Nothing will change in your life unless you want it to change. The Lord is a gentleman, and never forces Himself upon you. The Lord's love for you is tender. When you place yourself in the hands of the world, you will become beaten, bloody, and bruised. But when you place yourself in the hands of the Lord, you will be healed and made new. Whenever you walk in the ways of the world, you will be harmed, because of the injuries that the world inflicts upon you.

Jesus allowed Himself to be bloodied for you. He allowed Himself to be beaten and battered by the world, so that you could walk in peace and safety. Jesus allowed Himself to be imprisoned, so that you would never have to be a prisoner. He allowed Himself to be bound, so that you could be free. He allowed Himself to receive punishment for all sin, so that you could walk in the forgiveness of your sins. Jesus allowed Himself to be destroyed by the world, so that you would never have to be destroyed by this world.

Here is my question to you, my friend: Is the world destroying you? Are you bound by sin? Do you feel like you are wrapped in chains and you are a prisoner? Are you looking for a way of escape? Do you want to be set free from sin? Do you want things to change in your life? Do you desire to know exactly who He is? Are ready for Divine Deliverance in your life? He will deliver you, I promise you that, if you truly desire to be delivered. He is the key to your freedom--the *only* key to your freedom!

If I handed you my house key and told you to go open the front door to your house, would it open your door? Of course not, because my key is the wrong key for your door. You could try to put my key in every which way, but it would never open your front door. All of your energy, all of your efforts, would be for nothing. You must have the *right key*, in order to open your front door. No other key will work. And it's the same with your life; you must have the right key. Jesus is the key to your freedom, and it is as simple as that; He is the key to your life, the key to your heart.

But even without the right key to your home, I could break into your home, come inside, and steal your precious possessions. I would be entering as a thief, but I could do it. I could break in and destroy everything that is dear to you, devastating your life. I would have to watch you and make a plan. I would need a scheme to make sure you are not aware of my breaking in; perhaps I would creep in while you are sleeping, or preoccupied with other things. If I watched you long enough, I would learn your routine, your areas of weakness, and then I could make a plan as to how to distract you. I would learn about you and watch and wait. And then, at just the right time, I would come into your home, when you least expect it, and I would shatter your life by stealing precious things from you. I am a clever thief, and I don't need to be that strong, as long as I know your areas of weakness. Since you are unaware that I am your enemy and planning to harm you, stealing from you and destroying your life will not be difficult.

*"The thief does not come except to steal, and to kill, and to destroy."* John 10:10a *(NKJV)*

*Be sober, be vigilant; because your adversary the devil walks about like a roaring lion, seeking whom he may devour.* 1 Peter 5:8 *(NKJV)*

Friends, this imaginary story is meant to show you the mind of our enemy. He will sneak up on you when you don't even know anyone is trying to harm you! Be attentive; be aware of what is taking place in your life concerning sin. As we sin, and continue to sin, our sin grows; that is a spiritual principle that we must all embrace. Sin is not a game. It will eventually destroy and devastate you. Be aware of what is taking place in your life and notice the ways of your flesh. Know that if you feed your flesh, it will want more and more. Be aware of the ways of the enemy. He is watching you. He wants to destroy you. He is looking for areas of weakness in your life, so that he can come in and ruin you.

Some give the enemy a lot more credit than he deserves. He is not really powerful, but I believe he is clever. The Word tells us that when we finally see him, we are just going to laugh at him. He is a little runt. We are going to look at him as if to say, "This is the one?"

*Those who see you will gaze at you, and consider you, saying: 'Is this the man who made the earth tremble, who shook kingdoms, Who made the world as a wilderness and destroyed its cities, who did not open the house of his prisoners?* Isaiah 14:16-17 *(NKJV)*

The enemy is not that powerful, but when we allow our flesh to be stronger than our spirit, we are giving him a very powerful tool to work with in his efforts to destroy our lives. Cunningly, the enemy uses the desires of our own flesh to destroy us.

Our flesh may tell us these things about sex: Sex makes me feel exhilarated. Sex makes me feel good and it is very enticing. Sex makes me feel loved and wanted. Sex makes me feel like someone cares. Sex makes me feel like I am worth something to someone. Sex makes me feel in control and gives me power in my life.

But our flesh may instead tell us these things about sex: Sex is harmful. It makes me feel unworthy and abused. Illicit sex makes me feel out of control. Sex makes me feel numb. It makes me feel dirty, ashamed, and used. Sex makes me feel like I will never be loved by anyone. It makes me feel like a possession.

As I glance at the two paragraphs above that I have just written, I realize that I felt all of those things about sex within that three year period that sexual sin reigned in my life. And seeking to satisfy my flesh, I allowed the enemy to break into my home and destroy my most precious possession--my heart. If the enemy can destroy your heart, then he can destroy your marriage and your home.

Everything comes down to the matters of our heart. My heart experienced and was affected by every fantasy that was fed into my mind and every pornographic video that I watched. My heart responded to the sexual devices brought into my home and the other people my husband brought into our physical relationship. My heart endured as I committed adultery and as I was being raped. My heart was beating through every moment, through every sin, and it could not experience all this without being profoundly affected by these events.

*The backslider in heart will be filled with his own ways, but a good man will be satisfied from above.* Proverbs 14:14 *(NKJV)*

As my downward spiral of sin progressed, my heart became harder with each sin. The things that initially broke my heart into repentance, as I repeated them, ended up hardening my heart towards sin. My heart was soft at the beginning, but as I sinned over and over again, my heart became calloused by sin. Sin no longer felt like sin to me. Sin just became a word to me. I knew I was "in sin" but, "So what?" I thought. I did not realize the ramifications of the downward spiral of sin. I did not realize that the enemy was watching and waiting to destroy my life, and that with each sin the enemy was wrapping chains around me. It was not until I was already bound that I recognized my captivity. I did not realize how dirty my heart had become by committing these sins, until I desired to have a pure heart. We see David crying out to the Lord after he had committed sexual sins because David knew the condition of his heart.

*Hide Your face from my sins, and blot out all my iniquities. Create in me a clean heart, O God, and renew a steadfast spirit within me.* Psalms 51:9-10 *(NKJV)*

Sexual sins make our hearts dirty and our minds dirty. As a warning to you, in case my story hasn't been enough, I am going to outline for you the sexual sins that we see in The Word of God, with scripture references.

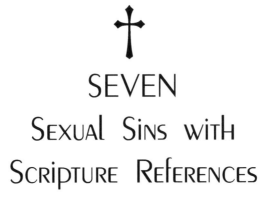

# SEVEN
## Sexual Sins with Scripture References

### Lust/Fantasies

Why is it a sin to lust for someone? Why is it a sin to have sexual fantasies? Why is it a sin to "just pretend" with your husband about different situations concerning sex?

Matt 5:27-28

*"You have heard that it was said to those of old, 'You shall not commit adultery.' "But I say to you that whoever looks at a woman to lust for her has already committed adultery with her in his heart. (NKJV)*

Proverbs 6:25

*Do not lust after her beauty in your heart, nor let her allure you with her eyelids. (NKJV)*

When you think about other people while having sex with your spouse, the Lord declares you are committing adultery with them in your heart. Whenever we lust for someone else, something very dangerous is taking place in our hearts. Yet the Bible teaches that we must guard our hearts because our life flows from our heart. Protect your heart to keep it soft and tender towards the things of God.

Proverbs 4:23

*Keep your heart with all diligence, for out of it spring the issues of life. (NKJV)*

Proverbs 4:23

*Above all else, guard your heart, for it is the wellspring of life. (NIV)*

Do not be deceived into thinking that you can just fantasize about other people without that having an effect on your heart. The fantasies will grow and the sin will grow.

Recently several best-selling novels have been leading women into a sexual fantasy world. These books have sold in the millions, because the enemy has tricked women into thinking, "This is just a book, just a romance novel. What could be the harm?" But reading this kind of material is opening up the door of your heart to the enemy.

If you are reading one of these books, I pray that the Lord will remove the scales from your eyes and that you will see clearly how dangerous it can be. I pray that you will realize that you do not want your mind entering the darkness where these books seek to take you.

## Self Sex

Why is it a sin to masturbate? Why is it a sin for a woman to have a sexual device and have self sex with it? Is it still a sin if a woman just thinks about the feeling that she is having during self sex, and doesn't even think about anyone while doing it?

This issue is very controversial in the Christian community, as I mentioned earlier in my book. Please allow me to share with you the things that the Lord has taught me about masturbation, which I prefer to call self sex. I was definitely in bondage to self sex. I could not stop having self sex, even when I desperately wanted to stop. Thankfully, the Lord delivered me from self sex.

Let me first state the obvious: we have self sex in order to have an orgasm. We want to have an orgasm because it feels good to our flesh--really good.

Here is the definition for masturbation in *Merriam-Webster's 11th Collegiate Dictionary*:

**Masturbation** *1 : erotic stimulation especially of one's own genital organs commonly resulting in orgasm and achieved by manual or other bodily contact* *exclusive of sexual intercourse, by instrumental manipulation, occasionally by sexual fantasies, or by various combinations of these agencies.*

Now look at the definition of orgasm, from the same source:

**Orgasm** *1: intense or paroxysmal excitement; especially, an explosive discharge of neuromuscular tensions at <u>the height of sexual arousal </u>that is usually accompanied by the ejaculation of semen in the male and by vaginal contractions in the female.*

It has to be concluded that masturbating is sex because the purpose of masturbating is to have an orgasm, which is a sexual event. In order to recognize that masturbation is a sin you must first realize that when you masturbate you are having sex. You have to admit that. Anyone who has ever masturbated knows that it is a form of sex, because your body is experiencing sexual arousal.

When you masturbate you are having sex with yourself, or sexual intercourse with yourself. You are lusting after yourself, or lusting after sexual arousal in your own flesh, and you are satisfying your lust by having sex with your own body.

As I have told you, I am married to a very sick man. Many women have told me that I should just have self sex because of my situation. The enemy has whispered in my ear and told me that many times. I am going to be completely honest with you, as I have been throughout this entire book. I did not have self sex for many years, but when my husband became very ill I started to do this on occasion, probably three or four times a year for several years. Each time I did it, I justified it within myself because of my husband's illness. I was always careful not to do it too often because of this verse:

*Stand fast therefore in the liberty by which Christ has made us free, and <u>do not be entangled again with a yoke of bondage</u>.* Galatians 5:1 *(NKJV)*

I knew that my periodic self sex could turn back into bondage for me if I was not cautious. So when I did have self sex, I was careful about the thoughts that accompanied my actions, and made sure not to do it often. I justified it with the Lord, telling Him it was okay because my husband was sick. "Lord, surely you must understand my situation," I reasoned. "I will not being doing this often, because I never want to be in bondage again." Though the enemy was cheering me on with this line of thinking, in the end my spirit recognized the deception, and that I was playing with fire.

The Lord began to deal with me concerning this and I began to have self sex even less often, perhaps twice a year; but I knew that the Lord was calling me to a much higher place spiritually. I had to stop compromising, stop attempting to justify my sin, and actually, stop feeling sorry for myself. I came to realize that the Lord wanted to teach me things and truly He wanted to give me the mind of Christ.

Over four years ago, the Lord addressed me in a very dynamic way, and I have not had self sex since then. It is no longer an option for me to do it all. I do not let even a fleeting thought of it enter my mind. I have learned to take complete control of my mind in this area, through the power of the Holy Spirit. He has taken me to a higher place spiritually, where He satisfies my every longing. *Jesus* is the lover of my soul.

I am not going to say that it is always easy, because it is not, or that I am never tempted, because I am. At times my flesh cries and screams at me, longing for that feeling. But when that happens, I have trained my flesh to just "Shut Up!" I am a passionate woman, but I have experienced a new passion in my life that I never dreamed was possible.

Whenever a woman has self sex her flesh becomes aroused. And when we arouse our flesh, our flesh grows and wants to become more active. At the same time, our spirit is weakened, because the strength of our flesh increases during self sex.

If I had been having self sex while dating Leo, my spirit would not have been strong enough to restrain my fleshly desires while in Leo's presence. I would have been arousing myself sexually during a time in my life when it was not appropriate to have sex with a man. Why do we think that self sex during our single days is okay? Purity as a single Christian means "*no* sex for now." Arousing one's flesh by having self sex will only make it harder to maintain self-control when you are with a boyfriend or fiancé.

We think we have self sex to satisfy ourselves and to make us feel less lonely. But that is a trick from the enemy, my friend. Actually, self sex makes you feel lonelier, and less satisfied. It makes you desire sex even more than you already do. It is feeding your flesh and destroying your spirit.

Romans 8:5-6

*For those who live according to the flesh set their minds on the things of the flesh, but those who live according to the Spirit, the things of the Spirit. For to be carnally minded is death, but to be spiritually minded is life and peace. (NKJV)*

1 Corinthians 6:18-20

*Flee sexual immorality. Every sin that a man does is outside the body, but he who commits sexual immorality sins against his own body. Or do you not know that your body is the temple of the Holy Spirit who is in you, whom you have from God, and you are not your own? For you were bought at a price; therefore glorify God in your body and in your spirit, which are God's. (NKJV)*

Be faithful to Jesus in your single days by not having self sex. He is your husband for the single time in your life. God will bless you mightily in your married days if you arrive at your wedding night in purity.

# Sexual Devices

Sexual devices are a counterfeit for the real thing. We think that if we play around with a device then we won't need the real thing. We think that if we play around with a sexual device we can keep ourselves from having sex outside of marriage. But these deceptive sexual devices make you want the real thing; that is, they make you want to have sex, even more than you already do. Sometimes, these devices deceive you into thinking that they can satisfy you sexually in ways that your husband cannot, and then you become less satisfied with your husband. You may even become tricked into thinking that your husband just can't satisfy you any longer, that you and your husband are just no longer able to have great sex, without the use of sexual devices when you are together.

God created man and woman to have sex together. God created our bodies to have sex with one another. God did not create us to have sex with man-made devices. That sexual device (the world calls them "sex toys") is an object--a form of an idol in your life.

Isaiah 2:8

*Their land is also full of idols; they worship the work of their own hands, that which their own fingers have made. (NKJV)*

1 Corinthians 7:3

*Let the husband render to his wife the affection due her, and likewise also the wife to her husband. (NKJV)*

Genesis 1:27-28a

*So God created man in His own image; in the image of God He created him; male and female He created them. Then God blessed them, and God said to them, "Be fruitful and multiply" (NKJV)*

The Lord will bless your marriage bed when you keep it pure. My second marriage bed has always been pure. These devices, which I believe are straight from the pit of hell, cannot even come close to competing with my second husband for pleasing me sexually. As I mentioned previously, the Lord can make your body do things that you never imagined.

Recently my husband saw a commercial on a network television channel that called these devices "marital aids." This is terribly misleading because although an aid should, by definition, mean something helpful, these devices emphatically do not *help* a marriage! God created man and woman with all of the proper body parts to have fantastic sex. True sexual fulfillment comes from having sex the way that the Lord designed it. Seeking sexual fulfillment with things created by man will never truly satisfy the longings of your flesh. You can trust me on this: I have been there, done that, and I know the truth about these devices!

## PORNOGRAPHY

Why is it a sin to watch pornography? Why is it a sin to watch other people having sex?

You cannot just observe pornography and not have it affect you. When you are viewing other people performing sexual acts, you are watching them sin and you are taking part in the experience. By watching, you are expressing agreement with what is taking place, and your heart is becoming harder with everything you see. Viewing pornography rapidly corrupts your mind, greatly strengthens your flesh, and deeply wounds your spirit. We must be so careful about what we put in front of our eyes.

Psalms 101:3-4

*I will set nothing wicked before my eyes; I hate the work of those who fall away; it shall not cling to me. A perverse heart shall depart from me; I will not know wickedness. (NKJV)*

Pornography is immensely wicked. If you place it before your eyes it will cling to your soul. The wickedness that you view will give you a perverse heart.

Pornography destroys marriages, and lives, and it will destroy your heart.

## Oral Sex and Fornication

Why is it a sin to have oral sex outside of marriage? Some people do not believe that oral sex is a form of sexual intercourse. Why is it a sin to have sexual intercourse outside of marriage?

Look at how the world defines sexual intercourse in *Merriam-Webster's 11ᵗʰ Collegiate Dictionary: 1 : heterosexual intercourse involving penetration of the vagina by the penis 2 : intercourse (as anal or oral intercourse) that does not involve penetration of the vagina by the penis.*

The Word of God tells us that fornication is a sin. Fornication means all sex outside of marriage. When a man and a woman have oral sex, outside of marriage, they are fornicating, just as when they have traditional sexual intercourse outside of marriage, they are fornicating.

Galatians 5:19

*Now the works of the flesh are evident, which are: adultery, fornication, uncleanness, lewdness (NKJV)*

The Greek word that is translated into English as fornication is the word porneia, which means illicit sexual intercourse (see *Vine's Expository Dictionary of Biblical Words* (Copyright (C) 1985, Thomas Nelson

Publishers). Illicit essentially means against the law, and all sex between persons not married to one another is against God's law.

The Word of God tells us not to fornicate and even the world tells us that oral sex is a form of sexual intercourse. So clearly, oral sex by unmarried persons would be a sin. Oral sex should only be performed between a husband and a wife if both parties agree to it; if they do agree, in the marriage bed it is not a sin. If the wife is unwilling, I believe that the husband should not force his wife to do this.

## Adultery/Group Sex

Why is having sex with other people, other than your spouse, a sin? Why is having sex with other people, even with your spouse's permission, a sin?

When we say our marriage vows we become united with our spouse as one entity (a couple) in the sight of God and man. When we make love to our spouse, our two bodies become connected, and we become one physically, connected to one another.

Genesis 2:23-24

*And Adam said: "This is now bone of my bones and flesh of my flesh; she shall be called Woman, because she was taken out of Man." Therefore a man shall leave his father and mother and be joined to his wife, and they shall become one flesh. (NKJV)*

Matthew 19:4-6

*And He answered and said to them, "Have you not read that He who made them at the beginning 'made them male and female,' "and said, 'For this reason a man shall leave his father and mother and be joined to his wife, and the two shall become one flesh'? "So then, they are no longer two but one flesh. Therefore what God has joined together, let not man separate." (NKJV)*

We have all heard of the Ten Commandments, and here is the seventh commandment of the ten:

Exodus 20:14

*"You shall not commit adultery." (NKJV)*

155

We know that adultery is a sin because God's Word tells us that it is a sin. Bringing other people into our marriage bed is a sin, even if your spouse is in favor of it, because God says it is sin. It is sexually immoral to have sex with anyone other than your own spouse. The marriage bed is to be kept pure.

Romans 13:13-14

*Let us behave decently, as in the daytime, not in orgies and drunkenness, not in sexual immorality and debauchery, not in dissension and jealousy. Rather, clothe yourselves with the Lord Jesus Christ, and do not think about how to gratify the desires of the sinful nature. (NIV)*

Hebrews 13:4

*Marriage should be honored by all, and the marriage bed kept pure, for God will judge the adulterer and all the sexually immoral. (NIV)*

## Homosexuality/Bisexuality

Why is having sex with someone of your same gender a sin? Why is it a sin to be bisexual?

In the Garden of Eden God created man and woman. He created the man first and then He created the woman.

Genesis 2:20-24

*So Adam gave names to all cattle, to the birds of the air, and to every beast of the field. But for Adam there was not found a helper comparable to him.*

*And the LORD God caused a deep sleep to fall on Adam, and he slept; and He took one of his ribs, and closed up the flesh in its place. Then the rib which the LORD God had taken from man He made into a woman, and He brought her to the man. And Adam said: "This is now bone of my bones and flesh of my flesh; she shall be called Woman, because she was taken out of Man." Therefore a man shall leave his father and mother and be joined to his wife, and they shall become one flesh. (NKJV)*

God designed a man and a woman to become one flesh. God did not design man for man, and woman for woman, to interact sexually with one another. We know this because the Word of God tells us this, and he calls homosexual acts shameful.

Romans 1:24-27

*Therefore God also gave them up to uncleanness, in the lusts of their hearts, to dishonor their bodies among themselves, who exchanged the truth of God for the lie, and worshiped and served the creature rather than the Creator, who is blessed forever. Amen. For this reason God gave them up to vile passions. For even their women exchanged the natural use for what is against nature. Likewise also the men, leaving the natural use of the woman, burned in their lust for one another, men with men committing what is shameful, and receiving in themselves the penalty of their error which was due. (NKJV)*

## INCEST

Why is it a sin to have sexual relations with a relative? The Word of God also clearly speaks against this type of sexual relationship.

Leviticus 18:6

*'No one is to approach any close relative to have sexual relations. I am the LORD. (NIV)*

1 Corinthians 5:1

*It is actually reported that there is sexual immorality among you, and such sexual immorality as is not even named among the Gentiles-- that a man has his father's wife! (NKJV)*

I realize that some women reading this may have been molested/sexually abused as a child, a teenager, or even an adult. Please be assured that it was not your fault this happened; you are still pure despite this betrayal you suffered. Take comfort in knowing that the Lord can heal you from the harm inflicted upon you in this way.

Sexual abuse comes in many forms and fashions, and in every single case there can be cleansing from the Lord. He wants to heal you completely from all of your hurt. You may be angry with God because you don't understand why God allowed such a thing to happen to you. We live in a fallen world that is filled with sinners who can bring harm to us. It is not God's fault if you have been sexually abused. Please accept that, and please allow Him access to your heart because He desires to heal you completely, and only He is able to do that.

## Bestiality

Why is it a sin to have sex with an animal? I'm sure some of you are thinking, "Why would you even go there, Stacey?" I address the subject because God lists it as a sexual sin in the Word of God. Since he does not ignore it, neither will I. In fact the Lord clearly directed me a few days ago to include it because there will be some women reading this book who have performed this sexual sin. He also told me to relay to those women that He loves you, and will forgive you of this sin if you ask Him for forgiveness. Do not allow the enemy to persuade you to doubt this. God earnestly instructed me to include bestiality in this book and He truly, truly wants the women who have committed this sin to know that He hung on the Cross for this sin too. He loves you and His Blood covers this sin.

Leviticus 18:23

*Nor shall you mate with any animal, to defile yourself with it. Nor shall any woman stand before an animal to mate with it. It is perversion. (NKJV)*

# EIGHT
## Getting Back to Innocence

### Broken Chains

As you know if you've read this far, I was bound in chains. I was in bondage to many sexual sins. I was a sexually immoral woman. "I WAS" and maybe "YOU ARE" doing some of these sexual sins currently. But "YOU ARE" can turn into "YOU WERE" in a split second. In Jesus' name everything can change! In Jesus' name chains will be cut in two, and bondages will be broken. In Jesus' name you will be set free, healed and made pure.

This book that the Lord has called me to write is coming to a close. I have spent many hours with you, sharing my story of how I dabbled with sin and gradually slipped into bondage in a pit of darkness. I've also shared how clinging to Jesus brought me deliverance, victory, and freedom. Most important, I've shared with you my Jesus.

What I hope to have made very clear is the downward spiral of sin—the fact that sin doesn't stay the same, it increases. If you continue to sin, your sin will eventually consume your thoughts, your heart, and your entire life. The darkness that you are living in will become darker; the depths to which your sin has brought you will become deeper. The consequences of your sin will become greater. The chains of your sin will become even heavier. Ask yourself if this is the life you want to live. Do you want to continue on this path that ultimately leads to complete destruction?

Have you ever seen a building being demolished by a massive cement ball that swings repeated from atop a towering crane? Each strike from the ball increases the damage to the building. The first crash creates a crack in the building. The second strike increases the severity of that first crack. The third impact causes pieces of the building to break off and fall to the ground. The cement ball keeps pounding into the building, and bit by bit, the building begins to crumble. Once the damage reaches a certain point, what is left of the structure suddenly collapses, leaving just a huge pile of twisted steel, chunks of concrete, and crumbled building materials. To me, that is a good illustration of the downward spiral of sin. If you keep sinning, the severity of your sin increases, and it will eventually reduce your life to a pile of scraps.

My life was demolished by sexual sin, growing one sin at a time. Oral sex before marriage led to sexual intercourse before marriage. Fantasies in the marriage bed led to use of sexual devices, self sex, and pornography. Pornography in the marriage bed led to sex with multiple parties and sex with both sexes. Bisexual acts with the spouse led to adulteries without the spouse. If we don't repent of, or turn from, our sin it *will* increase. And sexual immorality unchecked develops into sexual perversion. My sins were many and they beat my life into a pile of shattered fragments. But remember who holds the sins of the world in His hands?

Jesus Christ had a hold on my sins, when my sins had a hold on me. When I finally fell to my knees, He was there already holding me. He had been with me the whole time, and when I finally stopped pushing Him away, I could feel His embrace.

It is paramount to realize that *the battle begins in the mind*. Temptation, in and of itself, is not a sin.

Hebrews 4:15

*For we do not have a High Priest who cannot sympathize with our weaknesses, but was in all points tempted as we are, yet without sin. (NKJV)*

Jesus was tempted in all points but He was without sin. Being tempted is being human; there is no way to avoid it. You will be tempted by sin and that is a fact of life. What you do with that temptation will either give you victory in your life, or it could possibly bring death into your life.

James 1:13-16

*Let no one say when he is tempted, "I am tempted by God"; for God cannot be tempted by evil, nor does He Himself tempt anyone. But each one is tempted* *when he is <u>drawn away by his own desires and enticed</u>. Then, <u>when desire</u> <u>has conceived, it gives birth to sin</u>; and sin, when it is <u>full-grown</u>, brings forth <u>death</u>. Do not be deceived, my beloved brethren. (NKJV)*

The battle begins in the mind. Are you going to step out into sin or are you going to move away from sin? Action must be taken and the choice as to which direction to go is yours. God did not create us as puppets that He would control. He gave us minds and He gives us free will—the opportunity to make our own choices. What will you choose? You do not have to step into sin because our amazing God has provided a way out of sin for you.

1 Corinthians 10:12-14

*Therefore let him who thinks he stands take heed lest he fall. No temptation has overtaken you except such as is common to man; but God is faithful, who will not allow you to be tempted beyond what you are able, but with the temptation will also make the way of escape, that you may be able to bear it.*

*Therefore, my beloved, flee from idolatry. (NKJV)*

Through the apostle Paul, the Holy Spirit tells us to flee from idolatry. In other words, RUN! We must do something and God says the best action to take is to run away from idolatry.

Look at the *Merriam-Webster's 11th Collegiate Dictionary* definition for idolatry: *1 : the worship of a physical object as a god; 2 : immoderate attachment or devotion to something.*

Any sin that you commit over and over again becomes an idol in your life. Clearly you have an attachment and devotion to whatever is your addictive sin, so it qualifies as an idol in your life. You may want to stop, but you don't have the strength to resist it. It began as a temptation in your mind; then you stepped out into sin, and it has now taken root in your heart. You may already realize this, but let me emphasize that it is *much easier to flee from sin when it is a temptation in your mind.* Once you begin to sin, the temporal pleasure that accompanies the sin seeps into your heart. You know that physically your heart pumps blood through your entire body. Spiritually speaking, whenever you continue to practice sin, your heart causes sin to permeate your whole spiritual being; like blood, it seems to flow throughout your body.

To me, sin is very bloody. When I think of sin, I think of blood. Sin causes pain. Sin spiritually cuts us; that is why blood had to be shed to atone for our sins. Think of your physical body. Whenever you cut yourself, you bleed. His pure, holy blood was shed to cover all of our sins. Previously I conveyed what the Lord showed me concerning the movie *The Passion of The Christ*. "That is what your sin looks like on Me," the Lord explained gently. His blood says it all.

My friend, Jesus loves you. Jesus forgives you. His Blood has covered *all* of your sins. His mercies are new every single day. His grace is sufficient for you. My friend, *He* is your friend. He laid down His life for you.

John 15:13

*"Greater love has no one than this, than to lay down one's life for his friends."*
*(NKJV)*

Lamentations 3:22-24

*Through the LORD'S mercies we are not consumed, because His compassions fail not. They are new every morning; great is Your faithfulness. "The LORD is my portion," says my soul, "Therefore I hope in Him!" (NKJV)*

Are you bloodied by sin right now in your life? Have the chains of your sin dug into your flesh so deeply that you have bruises all over your body? Do you want to be set free from your sin? Do you want to be delivered? Do you want your chains to be broken In Jesus' name? Ask Him to break your chains right now. Go to Him. Fall to your knees. Cry out to Him. He is there waiting for you. He is already holding you.

The Lord brought me from sin to surrender. The Lord brought me from the edge of hell to the glory of heaven. When I hung up the phone after calling that married man, I fell to my knees and cried out to my Savior. At that very moment, my life was forever changed.

I urge you and beg you, do not pass up your moment with the Lord! Right now repent. Right now ask for forgiveness. Right now ask Him to be your Lord and your Savior. Right now be forever changed in Christ. This is your moment with Jesus. This is your Divine Deliverance!

Psalms 32:7-8

*You are my hiding place; you shall preserve me from trouble; you shall surround me with songs of deliverance. Selah. I will instruct you and teach you in the way you should go; I will guide you with My eye. (NKJV)*

The ending of this book can be a new beginning in your life!

# Early Response   A Poem

A woman who read my book before it was published, responded by writing the following poem, which she agreed I could share with you.

Set Free

I was in a prison with no way out.

I had no hope at all.

I was struggling daily to get myself free,

But I always hit the wall.

Then I heard a story of how

He held the key,

And through His Blood

I could be set free.

Who was this Jesus and was He real?

Did He really die for me?

So I fell to my knees

And there I prayed,

"Jesus I know I need you,

But I'm afraid."

"Please let me see You.

Please show me The Way.

Will You really be

With me everyday?"

There in the darkness I cried and cried.

Then all of a sudden I saw a bright light.

Jesus stood there before me with His arms open wide.

And in His right hand I saw a key.

I ran to meet Him and jumped in His arms.

What amazing love! My chains are gone!

Now I'm a child of The Father. I'm a child of The King.

Mercy, grace, and love have set me free!

By Joy

THEREFORE IF THE SON MAKES YOU FREE,

YOU SHALL BE FREE INDEED! (NKJV)

John 8:36

# The Lord Completes My Healing

In February 2012 my pastor was teaching at a leadership conference and at the close of his message he delivered personal prophecies from the Lord to several people in the room, including myself. He verbalized to me that the Lord has stored up all of the details of my life, even from the time that I was a little girl, and that the Lord has heard my cry. "The Lord has heard all of your prayers since you were a little girl," the pastor said, "and in a moment, all of your prayers are going to be answered." Naturally, these words from the Lord captivated my heart.

In the weeks that followed, I mulled over this message, trying to remember what the details of my life had been when I was a little girl and a teen. I tried to remember back to that time, when I was growing up in Alvin, Texas. I had no idea that the Lord was going to take me to Alvin, the place where I lived when this story you're holding began, so soon after these words were spoken to me. He not only took me there physically, but He took me there in my heart. He brought all of those details back to me. Let me explain.

I thought that I had finished writing this book, even though in my spirit, I just was not satisfied with the ending. I mean, how do you close a book like this? It is not a typical Christian book. I even mentioned to my husband that though I was finished writing the last section of the book, it just didn't seem right to me. It has been weeks since I finished the section entitled Broken Chains, which I had thought was the end of the book. I have spoken to my publisher and I have been preparing to send in my manuscript. Now, however, I have another God story for you, concerning the final section of this book. I was not satisfied with the ending, and there was a reason for that. The Lord had already planned the ending; He was just waiting to show it to me, in His perfect timing.

Our God is so awesome and amazing. He continually blows my mind! This book, my story, began in Alvin, Texas. Just this past weekend, I was back in Alvin to celebrate my dad's birthday. My dad doesn't live in Alvin anymore but he was visiting my cousins who still live there. My daughter Krystal and I, who love to take road trips together, made the 5 ½ hour drive to Alvin to visit Dad.

But this road trip was nearly cancelled before it started. I began to feel crummy Wednesday night when I went to bed. At work Thursday I continued to feel worse and worse as the day progressed. Despite feeling miserable, after work I made the thirty minute drive to the pharmacy to pick up the prescription medications my husband needed. Since I had to wait an hour for the prescriptions to be prepared, I went to the grocery store to pick a few things up. As I was checking out, a nurse I used to work with at the hospital approached me. She gave me a hug and asked if I could speak with her for a few minutes. We walked out to the parking lot where we had a fantastic conversation.

She opened up to me about some things she was struggling with in her life. I knew the Lord had opened up a door for me to minister to her, and I shared with her many things from this book. I shared God's Word with her and we talked for about forty-five minutes. At this point I was on fire with the fever, but also on fire with God's Word! Even though I was feeling miserable physically, I was so high on Christ that I didn't care at all. I prayed with her and we parted ways. We never know what ministry opportunities the Lord has for us each day, if we learn to listen to Him and our hearts are ready to serve (even when we are sick).

Driving home, I realized that I was really ill. I desperately wanted to go to Alvin to see my dad that weekend, but I knew that if I had a fever, it would be unwise to make the trip. As I drove through Harper on the way home, I prayed my pastor would be available at the church office, so he could anoint me with oil and pray I would get well quickly. Leo had already prayed for me over the phone, but I wanted to receive as much prayer as I could get. And the Word tells us to have the elders anoint us with oil and pray over us:

*Is anyone among you sick? Let him call for the elders of the church, and let them pray over him, anointing him with oil in the name of the Lord.* James 5:14 *(NKJV)*

My pastor *was* in his office! I tapped on his window, holding my oil in my hand to signal that I wanted him to pray for me. He prayed and anointed me. As I was leaving, I mentioned to him how sick I was, and he countered, "Don't say that. You are healed in Jesus Name!" I laughed, but I kept thinking about what he said as I drove away. Once home, I took my temperature and discovered it was 101 degrees. Immediately my husband helped me get into bed, tucked me under the covers, and prayed for me again. As I fell asleep, I considered my pastor's words, "You are not sick. You are healed in Jesus Name." Dozing in and out of sleep through the evening and into the night, I kept thinking about those assurances, and when I woke up my fever was gone! Although it doesn't always happen this way, I learned that day the importance of *really believing* that the prayers for my healing would be effective. God is always teaching me things and if you pay attention to Him, you will find He wants to teach and show you many things as well.

My daughter and I drove to Alvin Friday afternoon. As I said, the Lord had already planned the ending of my book but was waiting for His perfect timing to actually take me to and through the ending. You see, my friend, I grew up in Alvin, attending school there from kindergarten all the way through twelfth grade. The beginning of this book was set in Alvin, and it makes perfect sense that this book should end in Alvin. We serve a perfect God!

But this book is not just about me. In fact, this book is mainly about *you* and the work the Lord wants to do in your life. He is the potter and we are the clay. You have watched Him take me, a lump of clay, and fashion me into His image. He had a lot of molding and shaping to do, but He never gave up on me. He wants you to know that He will never give up on doing the same work in you.

*But now, O LORD, You are our Father; We are the clay, and You our potter; And all we are the work of Your hand.* Isaiah 64:8 *(NKJV)*

After my dad's birthday party on Saturday, I took Krystal for a drive around Alvin. I was showing her my old high school, the home where I grew up, and all of my old stomping grounds. As I was driving around, something began to take place in my heart and in my spirit. Memories came flooding back to my mind. Emotions began to well up inside of me and my tears began to fall. My daughter watched as this was taking place, and I thanked the Lord that she and I were together at that moment. Memories of the events and the innocence of my early years began to flood my mind.

I remembered sitting in the parking lot of the church where I was saved on that Father's Day so many years before. I now understood what was meant by the message from the Lord given to me by my pastor. I recalled the details of my life from when I was a little girl and a young teen; I remembered that my prayers at that time were for purity. My heart's desire was to stand before my Lord, without stain or blemish, to be His pure and holy bride. My relationship with the Lord as a teenager was very real. I was in love with my Lord, and yet I later strayed so far from Him, as so many of us do.

Why do we stray? Why do we walk away from God's perfect love? What is it that entices us off the path that leads to righteousness and lures us down the path of wickedness? Why do we turn from the truth and believe lies? Lies like the one that tells us that things of the world can satisfy us more than Jesus Christ. Those lies come from within our flesh.

If you are not convinced already, let me reiterate that our flesh is extremely powerful in our lives. It has the capability to take over our mind and change our whole thought process. Naturally, our flesh hungers for the things of a human, sinful nature; and when we feed our flesh what it wants, it grows and hungers even more. There is no way to escape our flesh. Since for now we live in fleshly bodies, the best we can do is learn to be led by the spirit, so that the flesh is not in control. As I've already stated, the stronger your spirit, the less trouble you will have from your flesh.

Remember my pastor's exhortation that the battle begins in the mind? For the most part, it is won or lost in the mind. Temptation is not a sin—we are all faced with temptations. The Word tells us we have great and mighty spiritual tools to fight the battle when it is still in our mind.

*For the weapons of our warfare are not carnal but mighty in God for pulling down strongholds, casting down arguments and every high thing that exalts itself against the knowledge of God, bringing every thought into captivity to the obedience of Christ.* 2 Corinthians 10:4-5 *(NKJV)*

When we generate sinful thoughts but immediately bring them into the obedience of Christ, we have won the battle, at least for the moment. When we *do not* take our thoughts captive to the obedience of Christ, and instead step out into sin, we are feeding our flesh. At that point we have already lost the first battle that was taking place in our mind, and we have entered into the second battle, which is much more intense, with graver consequences. It is the battle of the flesh. It is so much easier and less painful to win the battle in the mind than to win the battle in the flesh! I urge you, my friend, do not lose the battle in your mind. The weapons you must use for the battle in the mind are the ones I learned at the Crossroads class: prayer, praise, and the Word of God.

As women, we long to be loved and fulfilled. We want to be completely satisfied in all of our relationships, especially in that special, intimate one with a man. As a teenager, I began a relationship with a young man, and initially it satisfied my soul; he was my best friend. Our relationship grew in Christ and the relationship was satisfying to my spirit also. But as soon as we began to touch one another's flesh, everything changed. My flesh became very alive and *hungry*, and I began a journey of trying to fulfill and satisfy my flesh.

This journey led me to begin the downward spiral of sexual sin. The flesh will never be fulfilled. Oh, maybe for a moment it will feel satisfaction; but within a short time, the flesh will hunger for more. I lost my innocence. The purity that I once knew became a distant memory to me. Seeking to fulfill the lust of my flesh turned me into an impure, immoral woman. As I journeyed to the edge of hell and dangled my feet there, I was stripped of even the hope of being the person I once longed to be. I had longed to be a godly woman, and yet had become an ungodly woman. What began as just a game with my husband, led to divorce, and took me on a quest that resulted in my doing outrageous things in order to feel loved and cherished by someone--anyone. Would anyone ever truly love me? Would anyone ever be able to fulfill this yearning inside of me? Finally, my search to find fulfilling love brought me from sin to surrender. At last it brought me to the arms of Jesus Christ. He is my Maker; He is my husband.

*For your Maker is your husband, the LORD of hosts is His name; and your Redeemer is the Holy One of Israel; he is called the God of the whole earth. For the LORD has called you like a woman forsaken and grieved in spirit, like a youthful wife when you were refused," says your God. "For a mere moment I have forsaken you, but with great mercies I will gather you. With a little wrath I hid My face from you for a moment; but with everlasting kindness I will have mercy on you," says the LORD, your Redeemer.*

*"For this is like the waters of Noah to Me; for as I have sworn that the waters of Noah would no longer cover the earth, so have I sworn that I would not be angry with you, nor rebuke you. For the mountains shall depart and the hills be removed, but My kindness shall not depart from you, nor shall My covenant of peace be removed," says the LORD, who has mercy on you.* Isaiah 54:5-10 *(NKJV)*

As I sat in the parking lot in Alvin, Texas, with my youngest daughter, observing and considering the things from my past, I realized that God had brought me there to bring closure to the healing work He had been doing in my life over the previous seventeen years. Summarizing what the Lord had taught me, I shared with Krystal what I now understand real fulfillment is, and what genuine satisfaction means. "Jesus Christ, and He alone, can completely satisfy your every longing. The world is going to shout out to you, 'Come and enjoy!' but you must know, my darling daughter, it is a lie. Please never stray. Please never walk away, as I did."

My friends, despite my past, I know without the slightest doubt that Jesus loves me and has completely forgiven me. In His eyes, I am innocent and pure. *He* is the lover of my soul. *Jesus* is my fulfilling love! It's up to *you* to make him your fulfilling love as well.

**I say then: Walk in the Spirit,**

**and you shall not fulfill the lust of the flesh.**

**Galatians 5:16 (NKJV)**

As I mentioned in my book, I believe that the Lord has called me to write another book concerning the lives of other women. *Fulfilling Love* is my testimony, and I pray that it brought encouragement to you in the name of Jesus Christ. If you are facing an addictive sin in your life, please write to me. I will respond to you with truths from the Word of God to guide you in what you are dealing with. I fully realize that women need to know that they are not alone in their struggles, and that the Word of God has answers for them. If you have experienced victory in your life concerning an addictive sin, please share your details with me. Other women need to be encouraged through what the Lord has done in your life!

All stories will remain anonymous in the second book. Please give your age and the name of your city/town.

Please mail your story to:

Upward Climb Women's Ministry

P.O. Box 71

Harper, TX 78631

Or you may contact me through e-mail: staceylynn@staceylynn.net

Fall more in love with Jesus TODAY!

*The LORD will be awesome to them,*

*For He will reduce to nothing all the gods of the earth;*

*People shall worship Him,*

*Each one from his place,*

*Indeed all the shores of the nations.*

**Zephaniah 2:11** *(NKJV)*

# THE STORY BEHIND THE DOOR

The front cover of 'Fulfilling Love – From Sin to Surrender' was drawn months before Stacey Lynn discovered 'The Door' that is in her author photo. Through a chain of events that were taking place in her life, Stacey Lynn and her family had to relocate to another home in April of 2012. Two weeks after Stacey Lynn was living on her new property, she discovered 'The Door'. Shocked and amazed at what her eyes were seeing Stacey Lynn knew that this was yet another confirmation from the Lord, and that He truly called her to write this book.

*You will show me the path of life; in Your presence is fullness of joy;*

*at Your right hand are pleasures forevermore.*

Psalms16:11

*(NKJV)*

# Testimonials

The Lord has given this woman of God specific insight and revelation to be able to share her story in such a powerful way that His heart of immeasurable grace and mercy could be revealed. Thank you for sharing your journey of sin, surrender, forgiveness, and true liberty Stacey Lynn. Many Blessings!

Angela Davis

Young girls, especially young Christian girls need to hear the truth about sexual sin. After reading Stacey's testimony of truth I felt compelled to share it with my small group of high school girls. Thank you Stacey for speaking boldly and sharing your life so young Christian girls have the truth to fight the deception of the enemy.

Tina Reeder, High School Teacher, Calvary Christian Academy

I am 60 years old and have spent most of my adult life feeling as though I was worthless trash; my childhood confusion. Jesus guided my path, which brought me to read this enlightening book. I now have come to the realization that "I was a victim". Thank you Stacey for sharing your story. You have helped me to better understand and to move on. Thank you Jesus for giving her the courage to write this book.

Peggy F.W

Stacey Lynn's amazing willingness to just "tell it like it is", allowed me to just be honest with my own failings, fears, sins, and worries of a sexual nature. Her strength and encouragement throughout the book, gave me the courage to take my sins before the Lord and receive God's forgiveness on a real and personal level. For example, she defines "sexual sin" and gives clear-cut parameters and advice from biblical principles that answered many questions for me—questions that I could never have asked my pastor on a Sunday morning!

Stacey Lynn put a voice to the countless millions of women who secretly suffer from sexual sin and have no way to discuss deliverance. This book boldly announces that while this topic may not be considered acceptable to discuss in some church settings, our healing Lord and Savior is so loving and interested in us that He is quick to restore us and pull us out of the bondage of sexual sin. Maybe it is human nature to slink away from this subject, but Stacey Lynn challenges this belief and in fact believes that our precious Jesus heals and forgives even things we consider "unspeakable". There is true deliverance in our sweet Jesus! Not only does He forgive us but restores our hearts, heals our minds, and allows us to no longer be slaves to sin. Hallelujah!

Karyn Ellebracht

I was stunned by this book! Raised in a protected environment and unaware, this book shook me to my core! I think all women who are trapped in sexual sin and desperately want a way out should read this book. Stacey Lynn makes the reader realize that it is not hopeless and there is victory over this evil. The Lord's protection and forgiveness is always waiting there for you to reach out and take. His love is everlasting and He never leaves us no matter how we disobey. This was an eye-opener for me. Women of all ages and backgrounds will love this book.

Sheila Stokes

Printed in Great Britain
by Amazon